Gorgeous

Seeing Yourself Through God's Eyes

MANDY MUCKETT

Copyright © 2021–Mandy Muckett

All rights reserved. This book is protected under the copyright laws. This book may not be copied or reprinted for commercial gain or profit. The use of short quotations or occasional page copying for personal or group study is permitted. Permission can be obtained upon written request from Mandy Muckett.

While all the stories in this book are true, some names and identifying information in this book have been changed to protect the privacy of the individuals involved.

All Scripture quotations, unless otherwise noted, taken from the Holy Bible, New International Version®, NIV®. Copyright © 1973, 1978, 1984, 2011 by Biblica, Inc.™ Used by permission. All rights reserved worldwide.

Every effort has been made to seek permission to use copyright material reproduced in this book. The publisher apologises for those cases where permission might not have been sought and, if notified, will formally seek permission at the earliest opportunity.

All emphasis within Scripture is the author's own. Please also note that the publishing style does not capitalize the name of satan and related names. Choosing not to acknowledge him, even to the point of violating grammatical rules.

The Web site addresses recommended in this book are offered as a resource to you. These Web sites are not intended in any way to be or imply an endorsement and are correct at the time of writing.

This and other books by Mandy Muckett are available at Christian bookshops and distributors worldwide.

For any other correspondence:
Email: info@mandymuckett.com

Internet: www.mandymuckett.com

Book cover and interior design: Evangelista Media
www.evangelistamedia.com

Author's picture - back cover: Veronica Kiefer Photography
www.veronicakiefer.com

Author's picture - Styling: Loreta Schöpfer
Hairstyle & Face, Arlesheim, Switzerland.

ISBN 13: 978-3-9523254-0-7
ISBN 13 EBOOK: 978-3-9523254-1-4

For Worldwide Distribution

Dedication

I dedicate this work to the Spirit of the Living God, who led, inspired, and empowered me to write it. To the glory of Abba Father, Jesus the Son, and the Holy Spirit.

I thank my darling husband, Keith, and my daughters, Georgia and Sydney, who all gave me the time and space to sit in the prayer room at the International House of Prayer in Kansas City and write. I love you all more than you know.

Acknowledgments

The experience of writing this book would never have occurred if not for an invitation from my Pastor Silvia Nickelson; our trip together to the International House of Prayer in Kansas City, Missouri, USA, changed my life—and I really cannot thank you enough.

Everybody needs to be encouraged, and I want to express my heartfelt appreciation for the continual support and advice given by my close friend Martina Fink.

Always the consummate professionals who I now call friends, Clare Rogers, Esther Middeler, and Steffi Rapp have been and continue to be my guides and inspiration as a writer. I couldn't have written this book without you.

A prophetic word realized! Thanks to my photographer Veronica Kiefer for capturing my spirit in such a *gorgeous* picture for the back cover.

Last but by no means least, a great big hug to all of the women who reviewed my work along the way. Special thanks to Jane Webermiller who believed in me even when I doubted myself.

Endorsements

Mandy is the friend you always wanted: one who understands you, has been through what life throws at the modern woman, tells it as it is, and is disarmingly honest about her own foibles and questions. Through it all she shares openly how she has found freedom and answers by developing an intimate and vibrant prayer life with her Savior and Friend, Father and God. She tackles subjects such as the sense of emptiness, low self-esteem, weight issues, and family relationships. There is so much down-from-Heaven-to-earth wisdom here, and you feel you have gained a new and treasured friend as you read it. It should be in every woman's handbag!

Anne Coles
Anne and her husband, John, lead the New Wine organization in the U.K.

Anne is also head of New Wine's Women's Ministry (www.new-wine.org)

Once you start reading *Gorgeous*, it's hard to stop. It's a beautiful journey of an ordinary woman striving to be special—told with honesty, refreshing humor, and great insight. In her vain search for inner peace, she ends up on a dead-end journey until she finds the living God. The author's moving account of how she found her true self in God's love story inspires the reader to follow this call as well. Jesus says, "Then you will know the truth, and the truth will set you free" (John 8:32). If you read this book carefully, you will discover that Mandy's life and her relationship with Jesus—who is the Truth—changes over time and how the Spirit of Truth teaches her obedience in her walk of life. It is a learning process in which we become like Jesus and grow in our love for Him. I am touched with how Mandy is able to put her listening to the Spirit and her encounters with God in the throne room in simple yet compelling words that are so close to life. Her newfound freedom breaks through and reveals that we have this treasure in jars of clay and can journey from glory to glory! May her precious first book bring blessings and encouragement to many.

Lilo Keller
Co-founder of Stiftung Schleife, Switzerland
(www.schleife.ch)

Lilo is a passionate worship leader and author of
Prophetic Pearls

Contents

	Introduction	11
Chapter 1	Just the Way You Are	13
Chapter 2	Listen Love	23
Chapter 3	He Loves Me, He Loves Me Not	39
Chapter 4	The Garden Heart of God	53
Chapter 5	Consider the Lilies	63
Chapter 6	"Oh, You've Put on Weight!"	73
Chapter 7	To Be or Not to Be…	85
Chapter 8	Stop and Smell the Roses	95
Chapter 9	"Life Is Like a Box of Chocolates…"	113
Chapter 10	Your Personal Invitation	127
	Afterword	131

INTRODUCTION

I suppose I'm a typical English woman—as well as sharing the nation's obsession with the weather, I love to watch cooking and gardening programs. I love to spend a couple of relaxing hours, feet up on the sofa and a cup of coffee in hand, watching someone else's efforts marinating and baking or double digging and weeding. And I love to see the outcome of all that effort—the perfect cupcake, the perfect garden. The only problem is that when I get back to the real world, I can't help noticing that my own garden remains bereft of color, and my own house doesn't benefit from the waft of deliciousness.

My life is not all cupcakes and gardens, and that feeling of disillusionment when I switch off the TV represents some real struggles I've had—struggles with issues that I know many women grapple with. Life can be a continual battle with self-acceptance and body image, coupled with feelings of generally falling short compared to the images of perfection we see advertised all around us. The latest must-have beauty fad, accessory, or lifestyle gets paraded around as the world's answer to our deepest need—to be loved and accepted, just for who we are.

So why write about these struggles? Well, I guess it's because I know I'm not alone with my feelings of inadequacy, striving for perceived perfection and the approval of others, coupled with the fear of failure. I suppose my reason is to let you know that you are not alone. We all have friends who seem to have it all, who have "everything together," but I'm convinced that often behind these facades are women feeling just as alone as you.

And there are wonderful truths that I want to share with you—truths that will help you see yourself differently. I'm in the process of applying these truths daily to my own life. So please understand, I'm *not* writing from the perspective of a woman who has got it all sorted out quite yet.

My motivation in writing is stated clearly and simply in the following verse:

> *Praise be to the God and Father of our Lord Jesus Christ, the Father of compassion and the God of all comfort, who comforts us in all our troubles, so that we can comfort those in any trouble with the comfort we ourselves receive from God* (2 Corinthians 1:3–4).

CHAPTER 1

JUST THE WAY YOU ARE

My name is Mandy. I'm forty-eight years of age, I've been married for twenty-five years, and for the past twelve years I've lived in Switzerland. My husband Keith and I live in a small town called Muttenz on the outskirts of Basel, which is about an hour drive from Zurich. We have two daughters: Georgia, who is twenty-two, and Sydney, who is eighteen.

My life today is so different from the life I'd dreamed up for myself as a child. If we're honest with ourselves, we've all had dreams of what our lives might become. Every little girl fantasizes about the fairy tale life she wishes for, the "happily ever after"—whatever that means. For most, though, our dreams remain exactly that, a fairy tale, a fantasy. Our everyday lives are so far removed from our childish hopes. For some, the experience of female adulthood is overshadowed with pain, whether physical or emotional. For others, it's defined by an overwhelming sense of inadequacy. Countless women are existing rather than living; enduring life, not embracing it; living in a spiritual void.

Is this your reality? It was mine.

My early childhood was a happy one, as far as I can recall. Yet, even then, I sensed that I was missing out on something, something I couldn't define. I felt incomplete. I had grown up in a time when "God" was not a contentious word. Primary schools still had assemblies where hymns were sung and prayers offered, and harvest thanksgivings and nativity plays were the norm. I didn't come from a religious family, and no one I knew went to church, yet somehow I did believe in God. I wasn't sure what the word meant, but I believed in His existence nonetheless, whatever form that came in.

Looking back over my life I can now see definite times when God was drawing me to Himself, but I chose not to accept the invitation. I can remember church services I attended as a member of the Girls' Brigade (an international and interdenominational Christian youth organization). I recall feeling something as I entered the church, a something greater than myself, a presence that was comforting. In my early teens I briefly came into contact with a group of young Christians. I recall there being a tent meeting in the local park. I was invited, yet I stood just outside the flap of the tent door, not daring to enter. I just didn't feel that I belonged. Even attending church for midnight services on Christmas Eve stirred something within me, but I didn't dare follow the drawing of my soul.

I'd always had great expectations about my life. I'm not exactly sure where these came from, but I had them nonetheless. What I didn't expect was to meet, marry, and then fell in love with (in that order!) a tall, handsome black guy named Keith. Keith had expectations too. He'd dreamed of marrying a tall blond with long legs. Guess what? I didn't match up to his expectations either!

The years passed, and our married life rolled along a conventional path. We followed our careers, moved from house to house several times along the way, and had two beautiful little girls. Following Keith's career, we moved from his home town to Swindon, in the west of England. My life plan was on track. We had a big house. My husband was not only handsome, he had a successful career. We had a new Mercedes in the driveway, and all seemed perfect. Yet I still sensed an emptiness inside that would not be satisfied, however much I tried to fill it.

Around this time on British television there was a sitcom titled "Keeping Up Appearances." It was one of my favorites. The story centered on a matronly woman named Hyacinth Bucket (pronounced "bouquet"). In every episode this woman would attempt to keep up the façade that she was better than everyone else. She held candlelit suppers for those she wanted to impress or influence. Her life was full of materialism, elitism, and attempts at grandeur. I say attempts because ultimately, no matter how hard she tried to control her life, everything invariably went wrong—with hilarious consequences.

Unfortunately, my own life was becoming a real version of "Keeping up Appearances." I vividly remembered being single, pondering my fate if ever Keith asked me to marry him. My maiden name was Pass, which had spawned some unpleasant playground nicknames, and I'd dreamt of marrying a man with a sophisticated surname. Not Muckett! Mandy Muckett, I mean, really! But it wasn't a joke; it was my reality. I was Mandy Muckett, or Moo-kay as I might as well have named myself, a real-life Hyacinth Bucket.

I was overbearing and selfish, verging on suffering from obsessive compulsive disorder in relation to the contents of my house. I believed that I was on the road to either a nervous breakdown or a divorce or perhaps both. I was ripe for an emotional collapse. I lived with the growing tension between the reality of how I felt about myself, which I kept hidden from the world, and what I wanted people to believe I was. My identity couldn't be found in my looks as I considered myself average, nothing special, boring even. So my identity became intrinsically bound up with what I possessed, containing my fear within a lifestyle of control—whether control of myself, my environment, or the people around me. I spent much time and energy on accumulating stuff. I needed the latest trend in home décor. Even my kids had to be dressed in the latest cute offerings from the best "high street," designer stores.

My soul was desperate to be accepted, and if I couldn't attain that by my looks, then I thought I could secure it through what I owned. On the inside I had no sense of self-worth whatsoever. As for my relationship with my husband…well, I was very self-centered. I often joked that my wedding vows should have been, "What is yours is mine, and what is mine is MY OWN." I was prone to unspoken (yet noticeable) jealousy whenever other women showed an interest in Keith. In my mind, it wasn't *if* Keith would have an affair, it was *when*.

Being new to the area of Swindon, I thought it would be good to get to know my local community. I visited the small local library and found myself drawn to the spirituality section. Despite not being an avid reader, I took out a book about the Eastern practice of feng shui. It connected with my need to control my environment, and especially with the way I arranged my home. At around the same time I decided to take advantage of the opportunity to do volunteer work while my girls were at school or playgroup—obviously a worthy thing to do. I definitely would get brownie points for that! (Apologies to those of you who were in Girls' Brigade or Girl Guides/Scouts; no preference was intended.) My work background was in the English Magisterial Courts system, so I decided to use my knowledge to volunteer for the local Witness Support group based at the Crown Court. More boxes were being ticked off on my "life list." I was getting in touch with my spiritual side *and* being of help to my community too; that made me feel a lot better about myself.

The trouble was that these ticked boxes didn't really satisfy for long. My brief foray into feng shui ended up with me flinging the book across my bedroom. It told me that if my toilet didn't face a particular direction I was doomed to a life of poverty. What a load of rubbish! Was I really going to let the direction of a toilet dictate how my life was going to be? No way! I think that was one of those *eureka* moments, just like when the ancient Greek scholar Archimedes made a scientific discovery by getting into his bath, but instead of it being a bath, it was my toilet that spoke to me!

During my time as a volunteer, I had begun to make friends with a lovely lady called Sylvia Hetherington. I shared my toilet tale with her, to much hilarity. We agreed that the ideal position for a feng shui book was back in the library. Having done this, I came across the books in the next section: the religious section. I looked along the small line of books. Buddhism. *No,* I thought, *no more Eastern stuff for me.* Islam. No, again. I felt no draw to discover who Mohammed was. Then my eye fell on a little book titled *A Basic Introduction to the Christian Faith.* I thought, *Oh well, I know a bit about that, don't I? Baby Jesus and Easter eggs.* So I took it home and read it with interest. Some of what the book contained I had heard before, but most of it I hadn't; though to be honest, I wasn't sure that Christianity was really for me.

I told my new friend Sylvia I had gone back to the library and picked up a book about Christianity. She then confessed that she was actually a Rector's wife. I didn't know what a Rector was, but I accepted her invitation to attend the church her husband led. It turned out to be my local Anglican church, just around the corner from my home. *OK,* I thought, *that adds another tick to my life boxes; I could now properly tick the spiritual box too!* I enjoyed going to church and the sense of family. I regularly took my girls while Keith stayed at home on a Sunday morning to read the papers. What a good mum I was!

Or was I? As a young mother I suffered from a complete lack of confidence. I was a good administrator—I knew how to do that—but when it came to parenting I felt completely inadequate. My best attempts revolved around dressing and presenting my girls in a clean and tidy fashion. I knew nothing about playing with my children or enjoying them. They were just part of my life that I had to look after and keep tidy.

As time went by I entered into the life of this little local church. I made friends and started attending church events.

One day Sylvia invited me to attend an Alpha Course, a ten-week introduction to the Christian faith. *Yes,* I thought, *that sounds interesting.* So I embarked on a journey, which to date hasn't ended.

My experience during the course was extremely emotional. A box of tissues became my constant companion beside the comfy chair that I occupied every Thursday evening. Halfway through the course there was a whole day away, an extended time to hear about the Holy Spirit. On this day I was offered prayer, just for me—the first time anyone had prayed for me individually. I just cried and cried. (By now my little group was used to my copious tears.) When I returned home that evening, I read aloud a prayer, giving my life to Jesus.

I had huge expectations of this event. I actually thought that the skies above my head would open and that the very hand of God would appear over me. You may be asking, "Did that happen?" No, it didn't. At first I was disappointed; then I worried that I had not said the prayer properly. I must have done something wrong, as I didn't feel anything at all. I felt let down and ashamed at the same time, and altogether very confused. I didn't tell anyone about my embarrassing spiritual moment and life went on.

One Tuesday a few weeks later, I found myself battling with my emotions once again. As I've mentioned, my obsession with the tidiness of my house overrode everything else, including spending time enjoying my children. So when I saw four-year-old Sydney merrily jumping down the stairs, holding a plastic bag in which three delicate china bears were being tossed around, my temper exploded. The bears had been given as christening gifts and usually sat neatly in a row on one of the shelves in her pristine room. I angrily snatched the bag from her, scolded her, and stomped back upstairs to return the ornaments to their display position.

It was in the act of replacing the bears when I felt an overwhelming urge to take a closer look at them. I put the two smaller bears back on the shelf but found that I couldn't put the third down. I just stood transfixed by this china bear. Eventually I turned it over and was shocked at what I saw. Printed on the base of the bear, in bold black lettering, were these words: Mandy, I love you just the way you are!

I was so shocked I nearly dropped the bear. The words seemed to jump right out at me and grab my heart. I couldn't quite believe what I had read, so I checked the bottom of the other bears. They too had been manufactured with words printed on their bases but the cute lines didn't speak to me as these words had. It was as if I was hearing the very words of God spoken to the deepest part of me. To tell you the truth I was so freaked out that I immediately replaced the bear to its spot on the shelf and left the room. Not knowing how to process what had just happened to me, I tried to ignore it, and got on with my daily routine.

That Thursday, having buried the previous event somewhere at the back of my mind, I was struggling with feelings of inadequacy again. I felt worthless as a mother. I therefore decided to read a bedtime story to my girls—something I normally didn't do, but as good mothers read bedtime stories, I was going to rectify my lack in this area. But what to read to them? My eyes fell on a book of Bible stories for children, a christening gift to

Georgia, my elder daughter. I knew very few Bible stories, but I was drawn to one titled The Two Sisters,[1] the story of Mary and Martha, who each encountered Jesus in very different ways. Mary was the sister who spent time sitting at Jesus' feet just listening to what He had to say. Martha, however, was more concerned with the etiquette of the meeting, busily preparing and fussing around rather than spending time with her guest.

In the story of The Two Sisters, Jesus says, "Martha, Martha, you are worried and upset about many things, but few things are needed or indeed only one."

It was as I read the words "Martha, Martha" that I heard Jesus call to me, "Mandy, Mandy." In that instant my spirit came alive in me, a little spark of life rising up from a place that had been cold and dead. I had heard God's voice! I let the words sink into my heart, into my soul. God was there, He was real, He was alive, and He'd just spoken to me! I was speechless (and those who know me will tell you that this is quite something). My life changed at that moment, the moment I heard and believed in Jesus. I was then able to accept the words printed on that little bear declaring God's love for me.

If you had been on the streets of West Swindon that next afternoon you might have seen a red flash pass by. That was me in my little Ford XR2. Sydney was bundled into the car before I dashed, not paying attention to the speed limit I'm afraid, to the Rectory to tell Sylvia had just happened. At first Sylvia and her husband, Andrew, seemed a little bemused at my behavior and asked what the emergency was. After I'd calmed down enough to explain, though, they lovingly celebrated with me at my entry into the family of God.

And what happened to Keith in all of this? He became jealous of this "new man" in my life. He was used to being second in our marriage, as I generally put myself first, but he wasn't thrilled at the thought that it might be Jesus first, Mandy second, and Keith relegated to third place! However, he quickly began to see a change in me, and after checking out that I hadn't joined some kind of cult, he started attending church with us. Six months later, having attended an Alpha Course himself, he too gave his life to Jesus.

I have followed Jesus ever since hearing His words to me all those years ago. It has been an exciting journey. I've experienced the highest heights, the darkest valleys, and many twists and turns. I've often stumbled and fallen, yet God's Spirit has helped me get back up again and again. The idea of faith as a crutch to prop up those who are weak is completely inaccurate—following Christ is the hard option, not the easy one, especially in today's secular, humanistic society. But the challenge to follow Him is transforming me. This new life is worth all of the opposition I might face, and I am not ashamed to call myself a Christian.

If you are eager to open up your personal invitation to a relationship with God through faith in Jesus, wait no longer. Just skip to the end of this little book and begin by saying a simple yet heartfelt prayer. It's as easy as that!

Endnote

1. You can read this story in Luke 10:38-42.

CHAPTER 2

LISTEN LOVE

I wonder if you know a jazz track called "Listen Love," by Jon Lucien.[1] It's one of my favorites and I heartily recommend that you search it out and take a listen. Long before I ever picked up a Bible, its lyrics spoke to my soul about the need for divine love.

Though written as a love song, the words could almost be our words to God. I think of it now, because isn't God also reaching out to us, saying, "Listen, Love"? It's been said that in some ways, the Bible is a love letter to us from God. The Bible is a collection of sixty-six books, written by many different people, all inspired by the Holy Spirit to write. It includes various genres including history, laws, poetry, songs, words of wisdom, teaching, eyewitness testimonies, parables, letters, and prophecy. It's the very breath of God, bringing to life a library in one book, a book that continuously outsells any other written work in the whole world. All this is to lead the reader to its Author, to the very source of love itself: God.

I have received only one love letter in my life, from Keith, and it is something I will always treasure. He wrote it at a difficult time in our relationship before we were married, when I wasn't really listening to the voice of his heart. People may think of love letters as being filled with hearts and roses, but Keith's love letter to me—though romantic in part—also confronted me with my behavior toward him. It spoke of a longing to be loved in return for the love he lavishly poured out on me. In a way, the Bible's message communicates that same desire from God to us.

God is the ultimate communicator, and the Bible describes many of the ways He uses to make Himself heard, from creation itself (see Gen. 1); to a storm (see Job 38:1); a gentle whisper (see 1 Kings 19:12); dreams and visions (see Gen. 37:1–11); and even a donkey (see Num. 22:28)!

So if God is speaking, and saying to us, "Listen, Love," *are we listening?* How can we hear Him speak to us? It is our ability to communicate with God that I want to explore, this mysterious and miraculous communication called prayer. Let me describe some of my experiences to encourage you to take hold of this incredible privilege.

Being like Children

Hearing God is not difficult—we just think it is. Even the shyest children are not put off speaking to people because of their titles, job descriptions, or perceived status; they haven't yet accepted the preconceived ideas that we adults have developed over time. They see people just as they are, and I feel that this is the way Jesus wants us to be, as He said, "Truly I tell you, anyone who will not receive the kingdom of God like a little child will never enter it" (Luke 18:17). Listening to the King is a normal activity in His kingdom.

Could this be why it is often so easy and natural for new Christians to connect with God? As a new believer I often heard God speak, but I didn't think of this as prayer. When I thought of the formal activity called prayer I found it hard, but when I was not focusing on what I thought I had to do, I heard Jesus speak to me clearly. I can think of one example of this, during the time we were planning to move from the UK to make a new life in Switzerland.

At the time, we were members of the Vine Christian Fellowship in Midhurst, West Sussex. We had arrived early to the midweek house group we attended. As Keith and I sat in David and Christine Nickels' lounge, enjoying a coffee before the rest of the group arrived, I heard Jesus speak to me as if He were standing right behind me. He said, "Give them your car." The voice was so loud that I remember actually turning around to see if anyone was there.

At that time, Keith had a company car, and I had a new Vauxhall Corsa that I loved. During the home group I thought over what I had heard. *Give my car away? Surely not,* my materialistic self reasoned with me. *Sell it, perhaps. Then I could give them some of the money. Anyhow, what good would my little car be to a family with two tall teenage sons? They'd need a bigger car, wouldn't they?* At the end of the evening as we walked to our car I felt compelled to tell Keith what I had experienced. Keith stopped dead in his tracks and started to laugh.

"Why are you laughing?" I asked.

Keith turned to me and said, "Yes, Mandy, God told me that too. I'm just so surprised that you shared that with me!"

So the week before we left England, we gave the car to this lovely couple. They were amazed. We all cried—what a blessing that we could partner with God in His work. Unknown to us, Christine had been praying fervently to Jesus for a car. Despite her son constantly telling her that God just didn't give people cars, she trusted God for what they needed. Not only was a mother's prayer answered, but her faith in a generous, caring, practical God was confirmed to her teenage son, who had previously believed that the only thing anybody ever got from God was charity shop hand-me-downs. Jesus was given all the glory as this teenage boy told everyone, everywhere they traveled, that it was Jesus who gave them the car.[2]

Just as children grow and develop their language skills, so we grow in our ability to hear God. When we play hide-and-seek with little children, for instance, we don't make it difficult to be found, in case they feel abandoned and afraid. We wait in obvious places for the delight of the discovery, and rejoice with our children when they catch hold of us. My experience is that God is like this too. He delights in being sought after and doesn't make it difficult for us to find Him.

However, like playing the same game with an older child, being easily found becomes boring. I believe that as we grow in our ability to hear God, so He makes the hide-and-seek games more interesting for us. The ways in which we hear Him may change from simple childish chatter to what can be a most sophisticated and intricate exchange of hearts and minds. So don't be discouraged if you are not hearing God as you once had. It may be that He is just making the game more interesting, drawing you to seek Him in a new way; you will find Him just waiting to share in your delight. As it says in Isaiah 55:6, "Seek the Lord while he may be found; call on him while he is near."

My experiences of reading the Bible as a new Christian were few and far between, and at that time I believed that this really hindered me from communicating with God. I knew that I had heard God speak into my heart, but my everyday experience was completely different. I went to church, heard sermons, and sang songs to Him, but it was all so corporate—not personal at all. I decided that I must not be very good at this prayer thing. I obviously was not spiritual, knowledgeable, or faithful enough. Whenever I heard other people pray out loud, their prayers either seemed full of words and phrases I didn't know, like "binding" and "loosing" things, battling demons, and generally shouting a lot; or they were sweetly sincere and filled with words like "adoration and worship." The prayers that filled my own head were more like my weekly shopping list, and nothing like a conversation with the Master of the universe! So I felt inadequate and frustrated, to say the least.

I was fortunate, though, to stumble across certain tools to help me explore this mysterious thing called prayer, tools which have transformed my experience. The one that has helped me the most has been using a prayer journal.

Writing a Journal

As part of my spiritual journey, I had searched for different ways to connect with the divine. Prior to becoming a Christian, I had been an avid watcher of the Oprah Winfrey show. Other than interviews with the hottest stage and screen stars of the day, the TV program was full of advice from the latest self-help gurus. One particular episode suggested the practice of being thankful, and urged the viewers to start writing a "gratitude journal." I was immediately attracted to this activity as it meant buying a beautifully bound leather journal, tapping into my childhood love of stationery.

I still have this first journal and it makes fascinating reading.

As a typical new commitment, the first few weeks were filled with page upon page of heartfelt thanks. I was thankful for everything I could think of: husband, children, family, friends, home comforts—at the time of writing, the list seemed endless and that was even before I expressed my gratitude for the most basic things of life that most of us in the West take for granted. Yet as the weeks turned to months I'd found it increasingly difficult to find things to write about. In re-reading my later journal entries I was shocked to find that the very last entry only had these hastily scribbled words, "Today I am thankful for headache tablets!" Was this the only noteworthy event of my day? How sad. Looking back now, I know why my journaling stalled. The one thing that was missing from this activity, one that promised spiritual rewards, was that there was no focus or object to my thanks. Who in fact was I thankful to for all of the wonderful things in my life?

Thankfully, after becoming a Christian, I was reintroduced to journaling but this time as a focused spiritual practice, and for that I am especially grateful, as it has been one of the things that has helped me talk to Jesus. When I first embarked on using a journal to pray, the pages were filled with my "shopping list" prayers; but as time went on I began to open up my heart, finding the freedom to fully express my emotions through my writing. For a while the pages were filled with the woes of my life: self-centered moaning about my would-haves, should-haves, could-haves. Nevertheless I continued to write, in the assurance that someone was listening to all my rubbish. (After all, I could talk for England.) It's a good thing I was talking to patience personified—Jesus.

I have now been writing my prayers to Jesus for over fourteen years, and looking back at the entries, I am overwhelmed to see how far He has brought me. He has healed many of my emotional wounds, and my prayers are changing from an inward-looking shopping list to a wider expectation of what He desires. That is where I am now. I enjoy regular times of intimate conversation with Jesus, which I call my "cup of coffee times with Jesus." First because I am intentionally spending time with Him, just as I would with my best friend or close family member; and second because I do, in fact, enjoy a cup (or two) of coffee in the process. I usually journal in the mornings after the family has left the house, knowing I will not be distracted by the needs of others. Most days I also include a time of reading my Bible, and it is often during these moments that the Holy Spirit will illuminate something specific He wants me to learn. Frequently I am led to focus on a particular verse, or even a single word. I also often receive what I call a mind picture, a scene formed by the Spirit using my imagination. (Perhaps a story board or even a series of film clips in my mind better describes it.) I write down what I experience, and this helps me understand what I sense the Lord is saying.

Why don't you give journaling a try? Be intentional and carve out some time in your day just for you. That may seem impossible, but try to see it as giving yourself a well-deserved gift even if it is just a couple of minutes to breathe and plan or reflect on your day. Make your journal entries a means to an end, not just a depressing dumping ground that will lead to frustrations. Don't be over critical about what you write. Use what you have expressed to form questions to yourself and to God, then take time to listen. Not only will you gradually become aware of what your heart cries out for, but I assure you, you will begin to hear God's beautiful reply to your heart's cry.

LISTENING PRAYER

I've learned about "listening prayer" from the writings of my dear American friend and spiritual father, Dave Olson. This is a practice used by many to hear God's voice, personally, today. It is not a one-sided deluge of words but a real conversation with God. I'm just a novice, but I am gradually learning to listen more than talk. I nearly (jokingly) called this chapter Sheep's Ears—not to introduce you to a recipe for some Middle Eastern delicacy! but to guide you to Jesus' words in John 10:3-5. Here Jesus explains that as His followers, His sheep, we can hear His voice, be led by His voice and be able to distinguish the voice of the true Shepherd from those who wish to lead us astray. Over time, we learn to distinguish between the voice of Jesus, the voice of our soul, and the voice of our enemy, satan.

My experience, from writing down these conversations in my journal, is that when Jesus speaks to me, His words are always encouraging. Even if He is dealing with me like parents disciplining their child, His words to me are always loving. I have noticed that God's words have a very different feel to my normal spoken language, or to my own inner dialogue. It isn't that He speaks to me in some archaic language, but the words are structured in such a way that I recognize it as not being from my own mind. Discerning between my own self-talk and that of satan is also an ongoing process. I am increasingly able to sense that if the voice I hear is self-centered, then I am listening to my soul. The voice of the enemy can be deceptively easy to listen to, but this is the operative word: "deceptive." The devil's words never glorify Jesus or lead you to Him. They will always condemn and bring guilt, drawing you away to sin and his ultimate goal, death. However, when we hear from Jesus, we receive joy and peace.

We all need to hear God's voice, His heart's desire for us: to hear and know His love for us and His plan for our lives. Being guided by God's voice is available to us just as sheep are guided by the voice of their shepherd, yet for many it seems unattainable knowledge possessed by only a spiritual few. This is nonsense. Remember there are many voices that contend for our attention and, it is vitally important that we learn to hear from the voice of truth itself, God. So if in your prayer life, you have never heard what Jesus thinks about you, I would strongly recommend that you give listening prayer a go. A wonderful introduction can be found in two of Dave's books, *Listening Prayer* and *Hearing the Voice of God*.[3]

When I was newly married I can remember thinking that I didn't want to become like those old married couples you see in restaurants, sharing a meal without a word spoken between them. *How terrible,* I thought, *they must not be in love anymore.* Now that I'm older and have been married to Keith for twenty-five years, I see this situation with different eyes. Yes, the romantic love has changed somewhat, but the love that has taken its place is deep enough that words do not always have to be spoken aloud. That's what I'm after now with Jesus, to sit in His presence without the need to utter a single word. However, I'm not there yet. I still have a tendency to fill any silence between us with unnecessary chatter. It looks like Jesus will be taking me to a new level in our game of hide-and-seek; 3, 2, 1…ready or not, here I come!

Tongues of Men and Angels

First Thessalonians 5:18 tells us to "Rejoice always, pray continually; give thanks in all circumstances, for this is God's will for you in Christ Jesus." I don't know about you, but my soul answers that with, "Yeah, right, that's just not possible! Always? In all circumstances? I just can't do that." So how can we obey the Thessalonian text, even in our most challenging moments?

The answer comes in Acts 2 when the disciples received the promised Holy Spirit.

One of the effects of the outpoured Spirit was that the disciples each received a new language, either a human language unknown to the speaker or an angelic language. First Corinthians 12:7-11 lists the gifts of the Spirit, including this "speaking in different kinds of tongues." It's an amazing spiritual gift, and I would encourage you to ask God to give you the desire to receive it. I first became aware of this gift at a Christian conference. At first Keith and I thought the thousands of people at the venue were experiencing some kind of mass hysteria, so strange did it seem to us, but we soon realized that these people were experiencing something we didn't have. Their prayers soon changed into singing in tongues, many different voices joining together to create the most beautiful sound I've ever heard. To say it was like hearing Heaven was an understatement.

My experience in asking for and receiving this wonderful gift was unexpected to say the least. Keith and I had been invited to attend an evening hosted by the Full Gospel Businessmen's Fellowship International. The evening included a lovely dinner and a talk by a South American businessman who shared his story about meeting Jesus. At the end of the evening there was an opportunity for prayer. We were already late returning home to relieve our babysitter, so we decided that when people went forward for prayer, we would slip out quietly. But no, God had other ideas. As soon as we got up to leave, a gentleman came straight over to us to offer prayer. Being polite, we kindly accepted thinking it wouldn't take too long. After the initial niceties, the man asked if we had received the gift of tongues. Yes, said Keith straight away; no, said I, a little bashful, for it was something I had wanted to receive but hadn't had the nerve to ask God. So before I knew it, Keith had been paired with another person for prayer, and this man made it his mission to help me receive this gift right then and there. So shocked was I that I didn't have the nerve to tell this lovely man that I didn't have the time, thank you very much, but needed to get home. Oh no, it was as if his whole purpose that night was to help me receive.

Many people have fears about anything that is overtly supernatural in its nature, and receiving the gift of tongues is one of those things we might avoid for fear of being seen as weird. I too had some concerns but was reminded of the passage in Matthew 7:9-11, where Jesus gently says that if you "know how to give good gifts to your children, how much more will your Father in heaven give good gifts to those who ask him!" I also recalled what I had heard Jackie Pullinger, writer of the book *Chasing the Dragon,* say about receiving the gift of tongues: that God is not going to force you to speak by some spiritual possession—you can start and stop when you want to. If you want to receive the gift and use it, you first have to open it, and that means opening your mouth and starting to talk. And for me, with this enthusiastic man praying for me, it was as Jackie had said, I was just encouraged to start talking.

I found myself saying, not words that I knew, but just sounds. So like a baby learning to talk for the first time, timidly at first, I began to talk, my spirit talking to God. As an encouragement to you who desire to open this gift for yourself, I suggest that you first try in a private setting, perhaps in a time when you are alone with God, just you and Him, no pressure. Go on, rip off the wrapping paper and open the box! Your prayer life will never be the same again, I promise.

The wonderful things about praying in tongues is that it builds us up (see 1 Cor. 14:4). My experience is that praying in a spiritual tongue is of tremendous comfort in high pressure situations. First Corinthians 14:2 says, "For anyone who speaks in a tongue does not speak to men but to God." Praying in tongues is in its essence purely spiritual, my spirit speaking to God. It has allowed me to express myself when I couldn't even think straight.

I can think of one example of this, on an awful day when I'd just had a brief phone call from someone close to me. That person was on the brink of despair. He believed that his life was too difficult, that he had made too many mistakes, that nothing ever seemed to go right for him and that he wanted to give up living. The call ended abruptly, and I was unable to call him back. At that very moment I needed to pray like I had never prayed before, but I just could not form any rational thought. A complete sense of helplessness overwhelmed me. I have never been so grateful for the gift of tongues as in that dark moment. When I prayed in the language God had given me, my spirit was free to call upon God unhindered by my emotions or any other spiritual forces.

Romans 8:26 says it all, "In the same way, the Spirit helps us in our weakness. We do not know what we ought to pray for, but the Spirit himself intercedes for us through wordless groans."[4] I am happy to tell you that God answered my spiritual call for help in regard to this person and I was later able to give some words of peace and comfort to him.

I do hope that reading this chapter has encouraged you to pray. Prayer is a beautiful experience, and I truly believe that God wants you to know this beauty for yourself too. Numerous useful books have been written on the subject, but Jesus gave us the most famous prayer of all time in the Lord's Prayer (see Matt. 6:9–13). I suggest you revisit it when you spend time talking with God—you may be surprised by the power of its simplicity.

If you need structure during your prayer time, then the acronym ACTS can be useful:

Adoration: telling God how much you love Him.

Confession: sharing your failings with God, asking for and receiving His forgiveness.

Thanksgiving: expressing to God your appreciation for everything in your life.

Supplication: giving over to God all your concerns and desires.

So what are you waiting for? Jesus is expecting you! Go and have a chat with Him. You will be pleasantly surprised by what He has to say to you.

If after reading this chapter you now yearn to know Jesus and hear from Him for the very first time, why don't you take the opportunity right now to accept His invitation to come into relationship with Him? Just skip to the back of this little book; there you will find some simple steps that will help you start your new life of faith.

Endnotes

1. Jon Lucien, *Listen Love,* Mercury Music, 1991.

2. A few months previously, this same car had been stolen from outside our house, only to turn up a couple of days later without much fuel, but otherwise undamaged. I'd left a Bible audio cassette in the car, and I like to think that as the thief drove my car around listening to the Bible, the Holy Spirit spoke to him and his conscience was touched—or was it just a coincidence?

3. Dave Olson, *Listening Prayer* (Listening Prayer Ministries, 2000); and *Hearing the Voice of God*, www.inabba.org.

4. For further teaching on the gift of tongues, I highly recommend David Pytches's book, *Spiritual Gifts in the Local Church* (Bloomington, MN: Bethany House Publishers, 1987).

Chapter 3

He Loves Me, He Loves Me Not

Remember this game—He loves me, he loves me not? My little sister and I would sit in the long grass making daisy chains into crowns and necklaces, and tearing petals off a daisy one by one to the words, "He loves me, he loves me not." Whatever you said as the last petal was plucked told you if you were loved…or not. It was an innocent enough activity, but there was a shadow over it; the ache of the question, "Am I loved?"

Does that resonate with you? The awful truth is that millions of women all around the world are actually tearing at themselves, trying to answer the same question. Self-destructive behavior, even physical self-harm, is a desperate cry for loving affirmation.

This question is so much deeper than we expect. For the majority of us who have had our hearts broken by failed romances, the answer comes loud and clear: "No, he doesn't love you. You were wanted once, but not anymore." I remember countless nights spent crying over a lost love, my soul yearning for his affection, but being rejected over and over again. The curse on women really is the need of a man's affirmation: "Your desire will be for your husband, and he will rule over you" (Gen. 3:16). A brief brush with sexual molestation also taught my young soul how a female body can be used by a man for his own gratification, without anything to do with love.

My husband recently downloaded all my favorite "old school" soul records onto my iPod. Since I was a young girl I've been drawn to the heartrending lyrics of these Motown songs. The majority of our world's love songs cry over lost, betrayed, and unrequited love, and hearing them again immediately transported me to times in my life of disappointment in love. As an adult woman, married now for all these years to a wonderful man, I was shocked by the strong emotions the songs still evoked in me.

My meeting and falling in love with Jesus has answered that part of me that longed for the love of a man—Jesus being the only perfect man who would never forsake me. "The Lord himself goes before you and will be with you; he will never leave you nor forsake you. Do not be afraid; do not be discouraged" (Deut. 31:8). However, part of me remained that was still broken and in desperate need. You see, every women needs to hear the words, "I love you" from the first man in her life—her father. Countless women have never heard this. Is this true for you? My journey into faith came to a stumbling point when, having met Jesus in such a powerful way, the unresolved emotional conflict of my father issues raised its head.

I'd like to tell you how I discovered that the Father actually does love me. This discovery took place at New Wine, a Christian conference in England. I was camping at the conference for a week with my family, and I was on crutches, having broken my foot some weeks before. I had been a Christian for nine years at this point, but I knew that something foundational was missing in my relationship with Jesus. Over the past nine years God, in His mercy and compassion, had shown me so much about myself, my childhood, and how my life experiences had influenced who I was. My parents separated and divorced when I was a baby. I was about eight years of age when I was told that the man who I'd grown up calling Dad was actually my stepfather. In a way it was positive, because he wanted to formally adopt me, and our relationship was good; but from the moment I knew he was not my birth father, it felt to me as though there was a barrier between us. I met my birth father when I was in my twenties, but my relationship with him was nominal.

So, perhaps because of my experience of being fathered, there seemed to be a distance between me and God, no matter what I tried to do about it. I'd been baptized as a believer, attended Bible college, experienced the overflowing of the Holy Spirit, prayed and worshipped God in tongues, received loads of amazing teaching, been gifted by God to comfort and encourage others—and yet that feeling of distance remained.

At the New Wine conference, I spent a lot of time in the Prayer Shed, a venue at the camp where people could sit and take time to pray. I don't consider myself a diligent or skilled woman of prayer, but I know that Jesus always seems to want to talk to me. During three consecutive visits to the Prayer Shed, as I listened to God and wrote what He showed me in my journal, He took me on a journey that transformed my experience of Him as Father. The following is what I wrote on those three days.

A three day journey to meet Abba Father
Journal entry – August 2006

DAY ONE

On my first visit I sit in a large, comfortable armchair and try to still myself and concentrate—but I can't focus on anything. I open my eyes and look around the room, which has been carefully designed to help draw me into God's presence. It is quiet; candles are burning; a cross stands in one corner. Bread and wine, the elements of communion, sit on a small side table. I still can't focus. Then it's as if Jesus reminds me of how we have communicated easily in the past; I pick up my journal, and started to write out my conversation with Him.

As I write, God gives me a mind picture. It's of a vast landscape with a green hill in the distance. At the bottom of that hill is an old gate. A wooden cross stands next to the gate. On the other side of the gate there was a winding path leading up a high hill to an ancient castle, like a picture in a child's storybook.

In my mind I walk into the scene. I come on crutches having previously broken my foot; I feel burdened with guilt and shame from the past. I meet Christ at the foot of the cross—

His cross—outside the gate. I lay myself down, everything: my crutches, all of me, everything of me.

Jesus speaks to me. "I have an invitation for you," He says.

He hands me the invitation. It has my name written in golden letters on the envelope: AMANDA

(Amanda means "worthy of love." It is my birth name.) The invitation reads: "I have chosen you to come with Me to meet our Father. No adornment required; just come as you are."

I cry.

Jesus is the gate, and He opens Himself for me to walk up the path with Him—this path to the Father that He has always trod. The path is well-worn. It looks like white-weathered tree bark, or a smooth pebble that has been polished by the sea for an eternity.

I look up the hill and immediately think, *I can't climb it!* Then the words from Psalm 121:1–2 float into my mind: *I lift up my eyes to the mountains—where does my help come from? My help comes from the Lord, the Maker of heaven and earth.*

Jesus is there with me. He is in front of me, leading the way. He is beside me, helping me along. He is behind me, urging and encouraging me to climb higher.

I glance back to see the shadow of my old self: my past, my plans, my hopes, my dreams, my achievements, my failures, my fears, my schemes, my pride, my motives, my ego, my love, my hate, my indifference, my anger, my passivity. They are all below me, lain abandoned at the foot of His cross. The old me, abandoned. Abandoned by who? My earthly fathers! Abandoned by myself?

The new me is going to meet my real father. A child again—I'm a child again!

As I climb this holy hill I trust the hand I'm holding, the hand of Jesus. I'm looking ahead now to the unknown, the return to a home I've never known.

But…

I am known.

I am His child.

I am created in His image.

I am created for His pleasure.

My pace quickens and I'm surprised that I'm not as out of breath as I thought. I can see the door, so big, so solid, so awesome, and yet—so closed. I hear Jesus say, "Nobody comes to the Father except through me" (John 14:6).

I know that this statement speaks about much more than salvation. It's about meeting our Father.

Yet I don't worry that I can't reach the handle of the door. Jesus is with me, and I trust Him to open the door for me.

Day Two

The walk to the Prayer Shed this morning reminds me of yesterday with Jesus. I feel like spiritually jogging up the path to that big door. Last night I was thinking about what would happen today, how it will be so beyond my experience to meet "our Father." I have no framework of reference, and that's really scary, because I'm no longer in control. I choose to sit in a different part of the room today—a large sofa, all to myself—and start to write.

I take Your hand, Lord Jesus; lead me into the Father's presence, I pray. Jesus pushes the big door open with one hand. It glides open with such ease, not stiff from lack of use but graceful like an automatic door, a silent swish. I'm aware that I'm hesitating, resisting Jesus' leading. *Why?* I ask myself, and the answer comes quickly, *You haven't brought anything to give Him!* I feel like a rude dinner party guest who hasn't brought a gift, or a little girl wanting to bring home a good school report. I want to bring an acceptable offering, but have nothing to give.

Jesus smiles down at me. "You don't need anything where we are going," He says. Then I understand—Jesus is my offering! He laughs at my naïve need to please.

"Come on in," He says casually, like He's welcoming an expected old friend. I take a step over the threshold. *There, that's not as bad as I thought it was going to be,* I say to myself. I try to take in the enormity of the space I'm standing in. I feel paralyzed. I can't get any sense of the size or dimension of my surroundings. Yet I know this is a place of peace. *Guide me Lord!*

I feel like I've arrived at the ultimate adventure park but I don't have a map to follow. Where to go and what to do in this place is a mystery to me. I start worshipping Jesus in my head. I sing, *I enter His gates with thanksgiving and His courts with praise,* giving thanks and praise to His name; the words of Psalm 100 come so easily here.

I cry.

I want to dance for Jesus right there on the spot. I don't care what I might look like. I want to skip and spin in His presence, like a little girl wearing a party princess dress.

Jesus looks at me; His soft expression tells me He enjoys my singing and dancing.

"Enough now, Mandy," He says, "I've got more to show you." I'm surprised He calls me "Mandy." He holds out His hand and I take it eagerly, looking into His eyes rather than where He is leading me.

I become distracted from my prayer as more people enter the Prayer Shed. The interruption reminds me strangely of Jacob wrestling with God. As I wrestle inwardly with this disturbance, I'm encouraged to hold on to Jesus' hand. I say to Him, as Jacob said, "I'm not letting go until You bless me. I'm not letting go until You've led me into our Father's presence, into His chamber, His sanctuary, His throne room." I'm aware of a tighter grip to my hand. Is it me holding tighter or Jesus? I don't know. I read about Jacob wrestling with God in Genesis 32:28, when God calls Jacob "Israel." Do you want to rename me? I choose to believe that my given name, Amanda, fulfills its meaning, "worthy of love." Of myself I am unworthy, but Jesus makes me worthy to be loved because He chose me, He died for me, He gives me eternal life. I sense that Jesus doesn't want me to stress over the question of my name, so we move on.

Jesus leads me to another room, a changing or preparation room, where I can dress to see my Father. I came wearing a party dress, but I know I have to take it off.

I feel Jesus is asking me to undress before Him. I feel really awkward and ashamed of being naked before Him, of all people. He helps me undress, gently with loving purpose. I stand small and naked before Him. He smiles, but with a determined look on His face. He says, "I have to wash you now. Only once, and you will be clean forever."

He washes me; I'm covered with His blood.

I cry.

He cries.

"I've cleansed you with My blood and My tears," He says. "Now you are ready to meet our Father—go and dress quickly. He can't wait to see us!"

I dress in a pure white gown, like a long nightdress. The cloth is pure and beautiful; it's as light as silk, yet as soft as the skin of a newborn. I feel wonderful in my gown, just like I did in my wedding dress, but even better. It fits me like new skin. "I'm ready," I say, turning to Jesus.

"Let's go," He says, "It's time to meet our Father."

Day Three

I arrive at the Prayer Shed and I'm immediately plunged into anxiety. Where can I sit? The sofa is occupied and a little boy is sitting in the big armchair I had used before. I close my eyes.

Help me Lord, I can't focus. I don't feel comfortable sitting on a stiff chair. I can't get down to sit on the floor either because of my broken foot. Perhaps my physical struggle speaks about my spiritual struggle to come into the Father's presence. Jesus help me! The boy moves. I take the armchair and relax a little. I read the Lord's Prayer, yet my mind is blank.

Help me Jesus!

I feel tired and a little sick sitting in the chair. I'm reminded of feeling car sick as a child—the anticipation of getting to our destination quickly, to get the journey over and done with. Yet I feel this journey may be a slow one.

On my way to the Prayer Shed this morning I have occupied my mind with half-worded worship songs relating to the Father, but I couldn't sing a whole song through. I'm so tired, tired of the struggle, the struggle to father myself. I look for the story of the prodigal son. To my frustration I can't find it! I need the Father's word. I find it in Luke 15:20. It describes the sinful son coming back to the father. The story says that even though he was a long way off, the father came running to greet his son. I'm amazed, as if I've never understood the father's delight at seeing his son again.

Jesus, even though I stand with You on the mountain of the king, and within the temple grounds, I still feel a long way off from our Father's presence. Guide me, Jesus, show me the way.

I'm reminded of my relationship with the man I knew as Dad, John, my stepfather. I loved him very much but a distance separated me from him. Loving and being loved from a distance was my experience. How do I love and receive love intimately with my heavenly Father?

Jesus, You know how! You have the closeness to share Your thoughts with the Father, and He with You. I never knew my dad's thoughts about me, and he never knew mine. We couldn't and didn't attempt to share them. The gulf was too wide to get across. How lonely I've felt; how lonely he must have felt.

Jesus, I want to know the Father, to share Your intimacy with Him; to know His thoughts about me and to share mine with Him. Yet I know I can only do this through You, Jesus.

I take Jesus' hand again. He is taking me to another door. These verses comes to mind:

> *Ask and it will be given to you; seek and you will find; knock and the door will be opened to you. ...how much more will your Father in heaven give good gifts to those who ask him!* (Matthew 7:7,11b)

While searching for the story of the prodigal son I come across:

> *The Father judges no one, but has entrusted all judgment to the Son* (John 5:22).

Wow, I've never let that verse really sink in before. Our Father isn't my judge, Jesus is! Jesus, I thank You that You are my judge and that You have paid the price for my sins. It is You alone who hold the keys of the kingdom. It is You who died for me to give me life. Lord, I ask You to take me to meet our Father. Lord, I seek Your kingdom. I seek to enter the Holy of Holies, the temple of the Most High God. Jesus, I'm knocking on that door.

It's strange. Jesus stands with me on one side of the throne room door as I knock, and yet it's His smiling face I meet as the door is opened to me. Even stranger, it's not a door anymore, but a delicate sheer veil that He draws aside for me to enter. I'm made aware of the veil's transparent luster. I've been seen through this veil, yet I couldn't see through it from my side. I take a step farther. I'm covered by a substance I find difficult to describe. It's like being showered, engulfed, by a thick mist of perfume. I'm overwhelmed, completely drenched. I pause just to linger in this place, then I'm drawn forward, wading now through waves of what I can only imagine is God's glory, but I can only describe it as being like pure, heavy water. I feel loved in this place; it's extraordinary. The love seems to a take a physical form: the Father's love for me.

Forty-one years' worth of love just waiting for me to come and receive it. The weight is immense. I fall to my knees under its influence. I'm aware of my tears; my gown is soaked by them. *How long have I been crying?* I ask myself.

"You've been crying for forty-one years," I hear the Father reply.

I'm swept off my knees and am now prostrate on my face. I'm on the floor, yet I feel like I'm flying through time and space. I hear my name being called. I look up at the throne. I see seated on the right hand side of the Father, my beautiful one, my beautiful Jesus. He beckons me forward with His hand.

"Come on," He says gently, "Come and sit with our Father."

Even before I can finish my last thought, huge hands reach down and pick me up. High into the air I rise, being held aloft by an adoring Father, admiring His little girl; His creation; His, His, His.

He pulls me close to Himself. I can only say toward His chest, but it's not that; it's into His heart, yet more than that. It's into the world, no, into the universe, and still I can't explain this. I just can't give it expression. I give up, I give up. I give up trying. Trying to be what I think I should be. Trying to be what I am not. Trying to be my own parent. I just give up trying at all.

Oh, what peace, what power, what stillness. *How deep the Father's love for **me**!* I sing to myself. I know I will never understand. I'm not God. I'm not meant to be. I'm not meant to understand what it is to be God.

"But you are Mine," I hear our Father say. "And you are meant to know that I love you, know that I'm always here, and know that I've always been with you."

This place seems to throb the more He speaks, and strobes of what I can only call His glory pulsate around my frame. I hear Jesus laughing—a great big belly laugh. Jesus says, "Isn't Abba great, Mandy? I told you He was!" I relax, and for the first time in my life I feel me. I feel free to just be me. Fully accepted, doing and bringing nothing, just being me.

Any expression of thanks seems futile. I sense that He knows I'm thankful. I get the feeling that the response to this is to live my life fully in His Son Jesus. I'm laughing now, no longer scared of the Father but filled with childlike wonder. My God, my Father, my Jesus by His Spirit.

I'm standing again; I'm excited; I want to leave to tell others how awesome You are. I know I can come anytime with Jesus. So I'm not upset to be stepping down, away from the throne.

I return with the words of the Lord's Prayer on my lips, "Our Father, who is in heaven…"

My prayer is that these journal entries will be an encouragement to you, to know that our Father is ready to run out to greet *you*; that you'll meet a loving Father, not a judgmental one; that once you have met Him, your journey with His Son will never be the same again. You will be free to become who He created you to be, just as I am becoming.

As well as this spiritual experience, my understanding of God as Father has been greatly helped by Jack Frost's teaching.[1] His work on drawing people to the "Father Heart of God" became a significant part of my healing in this area. I urge you to take a look and see if the resources on his website can help you on that path toward the Father too.

ENDNOTE

1. Jack Frost's books and DVDs can be found at www.shilohplace.org.

Chapter 4

The Garden Heart of God

There was once a garden we have all heard of, an earthly paradise called Eden. This garden was a place of legendary beauty and the birthplace of Eve, God's last "hurrah" in all of His beautiful creation.

Yet Eden is the place we forever associate with Eve's fall. We all know the sad story of the forbidden fruit and that darn snake, ending in banishment from the Garden. All creation suffered the consequences of Eve's choice, the created separated from its Creator. (Though we sometimes forget that, in the biblical account, Adam was found to be just as much to blame.)

After His people were banished from the Garden, did God's love for humankind diminish? Not a bit. His love for us was and is unfailing, eternal, and limitless. Imagine His love being a beautiful garden, like Eden, but still very much in existence. This lovely place is vast, its size beyond our ability to comprehend—wide and long and high and deep (see Eph. 3:16–18). Once we were separated from His love, but God had already planned the way back. We can now access God's love through Love itself, love made manifest in the person and work of Jesus Christ. We have been granted admittance; we have access to the very heart of God Himself, into the Garden of the Father's love. This is what I call the "Garden Heart of God."

The relationship between the human race and God is compared to many things in the Bible. We are like sheep and goats (see Matt. 25:32) while Jesus is the Good Shepherd (see John 10:11). We are the clay; He is the Potter (see Isa. 64:8). In some of the most powerful imagery, we are compared to plants, especially grass: "All people are like grass, and all their faithfulness is like the flowers of the field. …The grass withers and the flowers fall, but the word of our God endures forever" (Isa. 40:6–8). And when Jesus describes us as vine branches grafted into Himself, the true vine (see John 15:1), He calls His Father the "Gardener."

I like to think of this picture of the Father as Gardener. It is much more true to life than seeing God as an old man with a white flowing beard sitting on the clouds, like some kind of Father Christmas in a long bed shirt. No, He is active and involved, carefully tending the branches of the vine with His huge, careworn hands, His love for us etched into the palms. "See, I have engraved you on the palms of my hands" (Isa. 49:16).

The Gardener God is an expert. The garden of His love is a place of color, every shade of the rainbow. His garden is both a place of order, in which He intimately knows each blade of grass—"Indeed the very hairs of your head are all numbered" (Luke 12:7)—and a garden with wild places. Not wild in the sense of disorder, but wild as in abandoned passion. The Father is an ardent gardener. His desire is as fierce as fire itself. He is passionate about you, even jealous for you. He declares over you, "For the Lord your God is a consuming fire, a jealous God" (Deut. 4:24).

A skilled gardener has a plan that includes each one of his plants. He knows his plants intimately. He knows everything about them, their characters, and what is good for them. Did you know that you were intended to be? You were planned; you were not an unwanted mistake. Jeremiah 1:5 says, "Before I formed you in the womb I knew you, before you were born I set you apart." If you don't feel that this is true for you, let these following words remind you of God's intimate knowledge:

> *You have searched me, LORD, and you know me. You know when I sit and when I rise; you perceive my thoughts from afar. You discern my going out and my lying down; you are familiar with all my ways.*
>
> *...My frame was not hidden from you when I was made in the secret place, when I was woven together in the depths of the earth. Your eyes saw my unformed body; all the days ordained for me were written in your book before one of them came to be* (Psalm 139:1-3;15-16).

If you can start to believe that you were an intentional thought in God's mind before the dawn of creation, you can then begin to take hold of the truth that there is a place for you in God's Garden Heart. In the garden of God's love, imagine there are billions of flowers, each one representing a woman's soul. Do you know that you have a place there, one that Jesus died to give you? Or do you feel like a weed, despised, unwanted and unloved? I declare to you that there are no weeds in the Garden Heart of God. In fact any good gardener will tell you that there is no such thing as a weed, just a flower planted in the wrong place.

Know that you have a place to fill in His flower beds, a place that cannot be replaced by anyone else. You are unique. God only made one of you. No one else on earth can fill the space made for you in His heart. Do you want to take your rightful place? The way back has been made possible for all of us. Jesus tells us, "I am the way and the truth and the life. No one comes to the Father except through me" (John 14:6).

When we choose to accept Jesus into our hearts, He comes to live inside us by His Spirit. The Father Gardener will water you with His Spirit. He intends you to flourish and bloom. He has so many promises for you, precious one, promises that are as true as His love, such as this:

> *The Lord will guide you always; he will satisfy your needs in a sun-scorched land and will strengthen your frame. You will be like a well-watered garden, like a spring whose waters never fail* (Isaiah 58:11).

Take hold of His promises for you as you take your place in the Garden Heart of God.

For my part, truth be told, I'm a fair-weather gardener. I should really confess that I am a lover of gardens rather than a lover of gardening. For me, the act of what I call gardening manifests itself in the occasional tidy up. I might randomly cut back a shrub here or there, or ask Keith to dig a hole for the latest garden center purchase. I'd love my garden to be full of color, a place that resembles the pictures in those glossy home magazines, but in reality my record in the area of plant care is pitiful. Ask my family—they call me the Plant Assassin.

You might be smiling at my family's name for me, but don't we sometimes feel that our Gardener God often acts as an assassin, seemingly obsessed with wiping us off the face of the earth? But I believe that what I lack in gardening skills, Abba Father has in abundance. You see the Father Gardener, unlike me, really cares for the flowers in His Garden Heart. All of His actions are out of utter concern for our ultimate well-being. Some aspects of gardening speak to me of the ways that He cares for us. We are fallen and in need of loving care, yet often we shun His attention because we wrongly believe it will be harmful and not of benefit to us.

The Compost Heap

At the back of my garden, behind our wizened plum tree, sits the compost heap. Keith puts the grass cuttings there, and occasionally I put in the broken bits of plants that I have collected in one of my all-too-few forays into the flower borders. Our compost heap is in desperate need of emptying. This job belongs solely to Keith, but I am always amazed when the miracle occurs—not, I hasten to add, the miracle of Keith actually emptying it, but what happens when it's emptied. From smelly, rotting matter has come the most deeply fertile and rich soil, full of life-giving potential. Dead stuff is made alive again. How can that happen?

As every good gardener knows, there are certain things that can go onto the compost heap, and things that definitely can't. The only appropriate place for diseased plant matter is on the bonfire. If its diseased parts were not destroyed, a plant would become unrecognizable as the gorgeous flower-bearing creation it was supposed to be. This disease is like our separation from God. Listen to what Jesus has to say about the vine and the branches:

> *I am the vine; you are the branches. If you remain in me and I in you, you will bear much fruit; apart from me you can do nothing. If you do not remain in me, you are like a branch that is thrown away and withers; such branches are picked up, thrown into the fire and burned. If you remain in me and my words remain in you, ask whatever you wish, and it will be done for you. This is to my Father's glory, that you bear much fruit, showing yourselves to be my disciples* (John 15:5–8).

The compost heap is a great picture of testing situations in our lives. Our Father Gardener will place us there to transform the smelly rotten stuff in our souls, over time changing us into something wonderful. He is strict; He will not tolerate that which could infect anything else. He has only one place for that stuff, the eternal fire. Examples of the diseased parts in a woman's life could be a toxic relationship, like an abusive, violent partner you have allowed to control your life, or a discouraging, life-sapping person you still believe is a friend. Are you poisoning your soul by holding on to unforgiveness, or do you continually speak negatively about yourself, thus acting out your own self-fulfilling prophecy? Do any of these scenarios ring an alarm bell in your heart? If they do and you feel like your life is a smelly mess at the moment, it may be worth examining the soil conditions of your heart. After telling the well-known parable of the sower, Jesus explains its meaning to His disciples:

> *Then Jesus said to them, "Don't you understand this parable? How then will you understand any parable? The farmer sows the word. Some people are like seed along the path, where the word is sown. As soon as they hear it, Satan comes and takes away the word that was sown in them. Others, like seed sown on rocky places, hear the word and at once receive it with joy. But since they have no root, they last only a short time. When trouble or persecution comes because of the word, they quickly fall away. Still others, like seed sown among thorns, hear the word; but the worries of this life, the deceitfulness of wealth and the desires for other things come in and choke the word, making it unfruitful. Others, like seed sown on good soil, hear the word, accept it, and produce a crop—some thirty, some sixty, some a hundred times what was sown"* (Mark 4:13–20).

Don't you want soil that produces a crop like that? If you don't have good soil, ask the Gardener to give you a spell on the compost heap. Go on, be brave! You may feel abandoned for a little while as the rubbish is dealt with, but remember the Father Gardener will not leave you there forever; it will take time for His mysterious processes to come to fruition, but transformed you will be. Just imagine the freedom you will surely experience if, for instance, you let go of a one-sided friendship in which you always give of yourself but receive nothing of value in return. Yes, you may feel lonely for a period of time, especially if you have enabled this person to fill your life, but you will soon be in a place where a new, more fulfilling friendship can be found. It will take time, but be encouraged, my love; the Father Gardener intends that you flourish and bloom. For we are "confident of this, that he who began a good work in you will carry it on to completion until the day of Christ Jesus" (Philippians 1:6).

PRUNING

Our Gardener God is very skilled at what He does, with every implement at His fingertips to tend His flowers…including a sharp pair of shears. We know that pruning roses, for instance, is essential to their care. Why, then, don't we appreciate the care that Abba is showing to us when we are spiritually pruned? I am currently in the process of being pruned. The Lord is challenging me regarding the amount of time spent and the content of my TV viewing. Time is precious and I believe Jesus has a better, more productive way in which I could use it. I do have to be honest here, dear reader, and admit that I am resisting this process. I guess this part of my life is like one of those thick, gnarly old branches in need of lopping off with a handsaw. Ouch!

Remember the picture of the grapevine? The Gardener's deep desire is that we produce much fruit, and not only that, but fruit that lasts. So when we are "cut back" by God it hurts, but we need to remember that He plans even greater things for us. I absolutely love sweet peas in a garden. This delicately beautiful plant can be a profuse bloomer, but to do this, its flowers must be picked regularly; the more this happens, the more it blooms. There's a great spiritual lesson to learn from this lovely little flower. If we allow our Gardener God to daily remove everything that is past its best in our lives, His Spirit will bring out still more of our beauty.

RE-POTTING

Every now and again plants may need to be put in pots. A pot can be a place of protection for new plants that are too tender to be put into open soil yet. It is a safe place for a plant to grow, but as it matures, this plant may outgrow its container, and its roots become pot-bound, at which point a gardener will know that a larger pot is needed.

Most of us don't like being too restricted, but I believe that God wants us to trust Him, and trust His ways. However we often rebel when limitations are placed on us, even when they are for our ultimate protection. The Israelite's rebellious reaction to God's commandments in Exodus is one testimony to that.

The re-potting process also has a lot to teach us about God's timing. When a plant's roots have no more room to grow, the gardener will put his beautiful plants into a bigger pot. Often this process can cause shock to the plant; its new environment is too big and overwhelming. I experienced this when God uprooted me from the security of my own country and re-potted me in Switzerland. What a shock to the system! But twelve years on, still living in Switzerland, I see that Abba had good intentions for me. He has given me space to grow.

Perhaps you feel you have long outgrown your pot and are tired of waiting to move on. God's timing is perfect, and He uses the seasons of our lives to produce a certain fruit that all of us have the capacity to grow: patience, one of the seven fruits of the Spirit (see Gal. 5:22). Patience is something we can't develop ourselves. As Jesus said, we cannot produce fruit if we don't remain in Him; and even if we do, it takes time. The Creator teaches patience to us as we learn to accept His seasons. He has set times for everything:

> *There is a time for everything, and a season for every activity under the heavens: a time to be born and a time to die, a time to plant and a time to uproot, a time to kill and a time to heal, a time to tear down and a time to build, a time to weep and a time to laugh, a time to mourn and a time to dance, a time to scatter stones and a time to gather them, a time to embrace and a time to refrain from embracing, a time to search and a time to give up, a time to keep and a time to throw away, a time to tear and a time to mend, a time to be silent and a time to speak, a time to love and a time to hate, a time for war and a time for peace* (Ecclesiastes 3:1–8).

Humans aren't very patient, as our supermarket shelves make clear. Thanks to the existence of worldwide transport, summer fruit is readily available in the winter. But nothing tastes better than fruit in season. Strawberries are for summer; they were created for summer.

So if you feel that you've stayed too long in the pot of preparation, I suggest you are right where our Father Gardener intends you to be in this season, a season of bearing the wonderful fruit of patience. So be patient, my love. Live patiently. For the Gardener God desires that you produce much fruit, and fruit that lasts.

CHAPTER 5

CONSIDER THE LILIES

See! The winter is past; the rains are over and gone. Flowers appear on the earth; the season of singing has come, the cooing of doves is heard in our land. The fig tree forms its early fruit; the blossoming vines spread their fragrance. Arise, come, my darling; my beautiful one, come with me (Song of Songs 2:11-13).

One of the most apt pieces of advice for women today doesn't comes from the pages of fashion magazines or daytime chat shows, pervasive and persuasive as they are. It comes from the mouth of Jesus. A man who was a carpenter by profession, living 2,000 years ago, doesn't exactly have the credentials you'd expect for speaking to the women of today—yet Jesus' words have stood the test of time, calling out to us across the millennia with clarity, strength, and simplicity. In Matthew's Gospel, Jesus talks about not worrying. He talks about our diets, about what we wear, about our striving to provide for ourselves. His words invite us to consider our true value. He proclaims our real beauty. He tells us that all of our efforts to attain beauty are not necessary because by seeking Him and His kingdom we will have everything we need.

Take a few minutes, perhaps with a cup of coffee or tea, to read His words to you. If you have time, I suggest you don't just read the words through once at normal speed, but try the ancient Christian tradition of *lectio divina*. Read the passage extremely slowly, several times, savoring each phrase. Then put down the book and enter into the scene of Jesus' words in your imagination, and see how they come to life:

> *Therefore I tell you, do not worry about your life, what you will eat or drink; or about your body, what you will wear. Is not life more than food and the body more than clothes? Look at the birds of the air; they do not sow or reap or store away in barns, and yet your heavenly Father feeds them. Are you not much more valuable than they? Can any one of you by worrying add a single hour to your life? And why do you worry about clothes? See how the flowers of the field grow. They do not labour or spin. Yet I tell you that not even Solomon in all his splendour was dressed like one of these. If that is how God clothes the grass of the field, which is here today and tomorrow is thrown into the fire, will he not much more clothe you—you of little faith?* (Matthew 6:25–30)

Do you hear His voice, the voice of the lover calling to our feminine soul? You may or may not be familiar with His words, but it's hard to deny that He already knew what the world would be telling us now in the 21st century.

Apparently, women can't move or breathe without the new next thing in fashion, diet fads, or cosmetic enhancements—all designed, so we are told, to make us beautiful. However they're actually all designed, first and foremost, to make money for those who produced them. It is primarily an industry for making money; its secondary aim is to make us beautiful. The beauty industry makes billions in profit each year. Its unspoken premise is that we need to be made beautiful because we are lacking and deficient and need to be fixed. We are not treated as if we are already beautiful—quite the opposite. We are told that we need the beauty that they have to sell us.

Please don't think I'm saying that we must throw away all of our beauty products and go *au natural*. I'm no different from most women. I too have paid credence to the latest fad (*paid* being the operative word), but I am asking you to take a moment to consider another opinion of your beauty: Jesus' opinion. Let me show you an amazing truth that Jesus showed me.

During a time of prayer I read those words of Jesus in Matthew's Gospel. I had heard them many times before and been touched by their powerful simplicity, but I still had so many hang-ups about myself. It's been reported that the majority of women, when polled about their lives, bodies, and so on, are dissatisfied with themselves in some way. Many actually say they "hate" certain aspects of themselves. I'm no stranger to those feelings. For many years I have fought and lost a battle with my weight. Issues of poor body image haunted me and my life has been a seesaw of emotions, from the heights of prideful denial to the depths of disgust and shame. I got to the point where I was tired of trying to be the "me" I wanted to be. Then I heard Jesus' words.

In a listening prayer conversation with Jesus, I asked Him about these verses in Matthew. In response, Jesus asked *me* a series of questions that I've coined "The Ministry of Flowers." The answers to these questions have transformed the way I see myself. I mean *really* transformed. It was like being given a new set of eyes to see myself with. This revelation is changing my attitude to my future, to the women in my life, and to the women I meet. I would love you to experience this as well.

Please take the time to ask yourself the same questions. Please don't just quickly skim this section if you don't have time; come back to it when you do have the time to give to God and yourself. This might sound a little melodramatic, but I don't want you to miss something important—even life-changing. Not that my words are any of those things—but Jesus' words are!

So if you are ready, find your favorite place, somewhere quiet and comfortable where you won't be distracted or interrupted. I know you busy mothers and businesswomen will be saying, "Fat chance!" but I trust that you can find one. Have a pen and paper handy, or if you're not such a techno dinosaur as me, your smart phone or tablet. Are you sitting comfortably? Let's begin.

In the last chapter I compared women to the flowers in God's Garden Heart. Thinking along these lines, the first question Jesus asked me, and He now asks you, is this:

1. What is your favorite flower?

This may be an easy answer for you—a no-brainer. Or you may have so many flowers you love, it may seem impossible to choose. Or you may not like flowers at all. I don't want to exclude anyone from this spiritual exercise, so if it seems a bit too stereotypically feminine, please bear with me and answer the question anyway. Take your time to ask Jesus to give you a mind picture of a particular plant. It does not even have to be an obviously flowering plant. Write the one or two that come to mind first, or that you connect with the most.

My favorite flower is: _____

So, do you have your flower? If you can picture it in your mind but are not sure of its name, don't worry. A picture of the plant could be a great tool to entering into a deeper revelation with Jesus. You could browse the Internet for the right photo; or for those who are creative, perhaps you could sketch, or even paint it. All I ask is that in some way or other you visualize the flower. Once you have chosen the flower or flowers and if possible have a picture, I want you to consider the next question:

2. Why do you like this flower so much?

What positive emotions does it evoke in you? Try to use as many positive adjectives as you can, rather than focusing on memories of specific times, places, or people. Please keep your answers as focused on your own feelings as possible. For instance, a friend of mine chose a fritillary. There are cultivated versions of fritillaries, but the one she loves is a wildflower, and she has only seen one in the wild, a single, delicate specimen growing in isolation deep in the countryside. She likes the fact that it prefers to be alone in nature, and although it's not big or showy, its isolation from other plants make it all the more striking when you come across it.

I like this flower because: _____

_____

The next step is to imagine that this flower you have selected as your favorite represents *you*. Imagine that when Jesus looks at you, He sees this flower. Then ask Jesus what He thinks or feels about it and what Abba, our Father Gardener's opinion is too. Remember, I'm not asking you what *you* think God's opinion is of these flowers; you are discovering what *He* thinks and feels about you. Just listen for His still, small voice, and write down what you hear, or at least what you think you hear. My friend with the fritillary mused on the qualities she liked in it, and finally felt that God appreciated her need to be alone at times, especially in nature, as part of who she was created to be; that this part of her character was not just anti-social self-indulgence, as she'd often suspected. She also felt that He had created her to be strikingly original in her way of thinking, and that He delighted to see this in her.

3. What does Jesus and our Father Gardener think or feel about my favorite flower?

Jesus' response: _____

_____

The Father Gardener's response: _____

_____

Remember that what you hear from God will always glorify Himself and encourage you. Anything you hear that is demeaning, cruel, or does not draw you to Himself will not be from God.

If you are having difficulty with this exercise, please don't give it up as a waste of time. I can testify how life-changing the answers will be. Seek help to listen; perhaps a close girlfriend, female family member, or counselor can support you in your journey of listening to the hidden places of your heart and the fathomless depths of God's Garden Heart.

You might be interested to know what my answers were. At the time of this prayer experience I had a narrow view of the type of women with whom God partners. All of the Christian women I saw in leadership at church or on Christian conference platforms were conventionally beautiful, feminine, manicured, and most importantly, *slim*. All these things, I felt, I definitely wasn't. I therefore assumed that this totally excluded me from any public role. Yet, I still had a desire somewhere deep within me to tell women that Jesus loved them, died for them, rose for them, and calls them continually into eternal life. Something was driving me to encourage women that there is a life to live, not an existence to simply endure. But looking the way I did, how was that ever going to happen?

The question of my favorite flower was easy for me. I love magnolias (the flower on the front cover, if you're not sure what they look like). The company my husband and I run together even has a magnolia as its logo. Why do I love them so much? The simple answer is that they are big and beautiful; they are impressive, yet at the same time they are so delicate that heavy rain can strip a whole tree of its flowers.

As I pondered my flower and focused on the picture I had, the Father answered me; I heard His words speak to the core of my being. Abba Father told me how He sees this flower, me. He said, "Mandy, a magnolia is big, yes. She was made to stand out in a crowd; she doesn't hide away, she is not hidden, and her beauty stands erect, boldly for all to see. Even from far away her beauty can be seen. She is gorgeous!"

Jesus then spoke to my spirit about the flower's special, individual qualities. He delighted in her delicacies, despite her size. The character of her coloring is subtle and gentle. She doesn't need a strong fragrance; her physical presence was sufficient to draw others.

Do you have a stirring in your spirit as you carry out this exercise? Do you hear the Father's deepest love for you, His individual creation? Can you hear what Jesus actually thinks and feels about you? Have you recognized what the Father Gardener has placed within you, even before you were born—the thoughts and feelings you already have about yourself, but have not acknowledged? His words are truth.

As you consider the answers you've received, let these truths about yourself sink in. Take time to start seeing yourself as He does. You are beautiful! You are a reflection of His beauty. You are unique; there is no other flower in all creation like you. There is a place in the Father's garden that only you can fill. Put your name where the flower's name is and say the words you have written out loud to yourself. Open up these new eyes you are being given and gaze in wonder at who you really are. My prayer for you: "Oh Lord, let any self-hatred be taken away—let her feel Your love today!" If God has spoken to you through this exercise, you could respond with these words from Psalm 139:14: "I praise You because I am fearfully and wonderfully made. Your works are wonderful, I know that full well."

It will take some time to start walking with these new eyes. You may stumble a bit. Like me, you may have many years of negative thoughts, ugly memories, and experiences behind you, which have molded your soul and self-image. However, in Christ Jesus these thoughts are *behind* you. "Therefore if anyone is in Christ, the new creation has come. The old has gone, the new is here!" (2 Cor. 5:17). Your past doesn't have a place in your future. You may have to renounce any terrible names you have called yourself. These are not part of the destiny of a daughter of God.

Jesus' ability to bless doesn't stop at a personal level. Since He has opened my eyes to see my own beauty, I am now enabled to see and appreciate the beauty of the women around me. It is transforming my relationships. It's not just the women closest to me, like my daughters, my mum, and my girlfriends; this flower ministry is helping me see past my fallen judgments of any women I meet. Most women, if they are honest, are the harshest critics of other women. We are our own worst enemies, and we'll often do the devil's work for him in crushing the beauty within not only ourselves, but others too. We often can't help but judge the women we encounter, either proudly elevating ourselves above those we consider to be less good-looking, or wallowing in pitiful envy of those we consider more acceptable, more attractive, or downright sexier.

My eldest daughter, Georgia, loves water lilies. I find this interesting because these flowers have similar characteristics to magnolias (I know that most daughters balk at the thought of being compared to their mothers, but it was wonderful for me to notice our similarities!). As for Sydney, my younger daughter, her favorite flower is a bluebell. Her flower comes alive when it's in its natural habitat with multitudes of others, like the carpets of brilliant bluebells that fill English woodlands in the spring. By her own admission, Sydney loves being with people and comes alive when she is helping others.

The most surprising outcome of this ministry has been what Jesus has shown me about my own mother. As with many mother-daughter relationships, ours is complex and I haven't always appreciated her for who she is. My mother has two favorite plants. The first is tropical: the anthurium has a huge red waxy heart-shaped flower with a large tongue-like form at its center. Those who know my mum know her generous nature. She always has her heart in the right place, her intentions always other-centered. But there is a little rebel living in her, like a little girl cheekily sticking out her tongue at the world, just like the tongue in the heart of her favorite flower. That's the mum I know!

Her other flower is a type of orchid. When she explained to me why she loved them so much, her words took my breath away. She said, "You have to look inside to see their beauty!" That statement caught me off-guard. It was as if Jesus was saying to me, "Mandy, you have to look deep within your mother to see the beauty I've put there." How humbling, revealing, and true. I now see your inner beauty, Mum, and I do love you!

Chapter 6

"Oh, You've Put on Weight!"

Picture this scene in your mind: a long-awaited holiday on an exotic Caribbean island with the warm, turquoise sea lapping lazy waves onto a pristine beach. It is early on a Sunday morning and a gentle breeze is stirring the leaves of the coconut palms as I walk with my husband and his parents to attend the local church. It is like a little bit of Heaven on earth.

We enter the cool interior of an old, gray stone, castle-like building and find a seat on one of the polished wooden pews. Life was good and all was well in my world until I heard the words that floated up the aisle in my direction, "Oh, you've put on weight!"—my perfect piece of paradise, shattered by one simple sentence.

My little story describes our first trip to visit Keith's parents, Ken and Linda, who had retired in England and returned to their home in Saint Vincent and the Grenadines, a small island not too distant from the popular tourist destination of Saint Lucia. This woman, a family friend who had attended our wedding in England many years before, had taken the opportunity before the service to come over and greet us—what a greeting!

A simple statement of fact would have, for most people, remained a guarded thought, but in this case it burst out of this woman like a cork from a bottle of champagne, with no consideration as to the filter of politeness or with regard to its emotional impact. No, I received her factual statement as if I had been hit by the bullets from a double-barreled shot gun fired at close range. Ouch! Woman down! These surely are the words no woman ever wants to hear.

Here's another extract from my prayer journal, where God addressed the vanity of self and my own perception of my image rather than God's view of me. As I sat under the pergola in my garden, journaling on a beautiful sunny afternoon, the Holy Spirit gave me a picture in my mind of an old fashioned fairground with a big carousel, rides, and sideshows. This was the setting He gave me to explore what God wanted to show me.

The Hall of Mirrors: Deception and Lies
Journal entry – June 2007

I close my eyes and God's Spirit shows me that I'm walking with Jesus around a fairground. I'm drawn by the glint of the sign above the Hall of Mirrors. I can see people inside, walking around in what appears to be a glass maze. They seem to be having fun, and I want to go in. I hesitate, then think, *It's all right—it's not scary like a rollercoaster. I can go and see what it's like inside and come out whenever I want.*

I let go of Jesus' hand, not thinking to ask His opinion. I push against the revolving turnstile and step into the maze. I feel completely safe; I can still see Jesus waiting for me outside the entrance to the maze. He is just standing on the other side of the glass. I can also see the exit at the end of the maze. This looks so easy. I just have to find my way through to the end. The maze is made up of clear glass and mirror doors. I push a door, and it opens up into a space with more doors to choose from. *Yes,* I say to myself, *just head in the right direction, and I'll be through in no time.* I push through a second door into a corridor of mirrors. As I walk along I notice my outline contort in the convex and concave mirrors that hang on the walls. I laugh at the way I can change the way I see myself—a long neck, tiny head, and short legs. I walk from mirror to mirror, trying to find one that manipulates my form into one I like—the one I'd love to have naturally. Wouldn't it be great if people could see me just how I dream of being—tall, slim, and long-legged?

These mirrors, you see, represent the world's unrealistic expectations of how we should look, as well as our own vain desire to be accepted by others. We all know how, in real life, computer images of even top fashion models are digitally enhanced to fit the world's idea of perfection.

Then I come to a normal mirror where I'm confronted by my real image. Oh what disappointment I see in my face. I turn away, disgusted. Fat, ugly, and a wonky eye to boot! Then I hear Jesus speaking as clearly as though He were right beside me, "Mandy, you are beautiful, My beloved."

How beautiful you are, my darling. Oh, how beautiful!
(Song of Songs 4:1).

I look back again at my reflection.

"How can You call me beautiful, Lord?' I ask.

"You are ugly, fat, and useless," spits the mirror, taunting me like a playground bully. I cover my eyes so I can't see the reflection.

Then I hear Jesus again, this time speaking to someone I can't see. "You belong to your father, the devil, and you want to carry out your father's desire. He was a murderer from the beginning, not holding to the truth, for there is no truth in him. When he lies he speaks his native language for he is a liar and the father of lies" (John 8:44).

I begin to feel claustrophobic, so I search for the exit. I push against a door, but it won't open. I push again. I can see the exit but can't get to it. I try another door and that too is unmoving. I feel panic rising, and try to calm myself.

"I can get out of here myself," I say, "It's easy." Oh, that self-talk. Why do I persist in listening to myself? Always wanting to go my way, and always ending up getting lost.

There is a way that appears to be right, but in the end it leads to death (Proverbs 14:12).

The sense of lostness is very disturbing; although I can see Jesus, who is the way out, I can't get to Him by myself. I can see the way I need to go but am being blinded by my own choices. I feel desperate now, trying to calm myself enough to think clearly. I recall that to get out of a maze you should always turn right…or was that left?

"Help me, Lord!" I cry.

I look up, and through my tears I see the blurred reflection of Jesus in one of the mirrored doors. He speaks to me again, calling my name, reminding me:

> *For now we see only a reflection as in a mirror; then we shall see face to face. Now I know in part; there I shall know fully, even as I am fully known* (1 Corinthians 13:12).
>
> *…If you hold to my teaching, you are really my disciples. Then you will know the truth, and the truth will set you free* (John 8:31–32).

His words saturate my soul, and I know that if I continue to follow His voice, His way, I will get home safely. I had lost my bearings as I gave credence to the world's opinions, values, and condemnations; now I know it was all lies and distortion, and the only one who is qualified to both lead and judge me is Jesus. A few more steps and the reality of escape lies in front of me. I stumble through the exit turnstile into Jesus' waiting arms, safe like a lamb in the arms of the Shepherd. Jesus whispers softly in my ear, "We all like sheep, have gone astray. Each of us has turned to his own way; and the Lord has laid on him the iniquity of us all" (Isa. 53:6). "'For my thoughts are not your thoughts, neither are your ways my ways,' declares the Lord. 'As the heavens are higher than the earth, so are my ways higher than your ways and my thoughts higher than your thoughts'" (Isa. 55:8–9).

Lord, I sin every time I go my own way, when I think I know better. I can truly say of myself that,

"If we claim to be without sin, we deceive ourselves and the truth is not in us" (1 John 1:8). Lord, You have freed me from the penalty of my sin: "For the wages of sin is death, but the gift of God is eternal life in Christ Jesus our Lord" (Rom. 6:23).

Lord, I ask that by the help of Your Holy Spirit I incline my ear to hear Your voice, to hear the truth about how You really see me, feel about me, and think about me. Help me to follow Your way and not my own, every day.

Having shared this experience I am struck by Jesus' interest in every aspect of our everyday lives, even those times when we go our own way believing we know better. He wants to be involved not only in the big stuff of life but deeply desires to walk every step of the way with us. With this thought in mind, perhaps we can take time to pause and consider His opinion more often, now knowing that when we do we surely can't go wrong.

Simply reading the Bible has spoken to me as much as any experience in prayer. I often feel I'm an inconsistent follower of Jesus, but I do attempt to read and study the Word of God regularly. The Bible tells us there is wisdom to be found in its pages; and one day a piece of Scripture addressed how I view and treat my body, as well as my relationship with food. It was a great surprise to me because it comes from a passage I've tried to avoid, a passage in First Corinthians that has been my nemesis for many years, particularly the words, "Do you not know that your bodies are temples of the Holy Spirit?" (1 Cor. 6:19).

These words were a source of condemnation for me. Whenever I brought my struggles with food and body image to God, this sentence would come into my mind time and again. And what it meant to me was, "Don't you know, you idiot, that your body is a temple of the Holy Spirit? Look what you've done, and continue to do to it!" I believed the lie that to be a better me, there must be less of me—literally.

Mercifully, I've learned how to hear the voice of God more clearly over time, and to understand the difference between His voice and my soul speaking. Most importantly, I am beginning to understand how satan uses his extensive knowledge of Scripture for his own destructive purposes. He really is the thief that comes into our lives to kill, steal, and destroy. He is "hell bent" on destroying us, by luring us away from our only perfect, eternal source of love and life. Jesus, on the other hand, only uses Scripture to lovingly show us the truth, gently removing the denial that clouds our sight and showing us the reality that will draw us to Himself in humble dependency.

Women have so often been condemned through the misrepresentation of Scripture, especially the apostle Paul's teaching. I've even heard women say that Paul was a woman-hater! This seems perverse to me, yet understandable since Scripture is so often read out of its historical setting and cultural context, distorting its meaning. I'm not saying that all Scripture is easy to understand or apply; plenty of passages remain a mystery to the most well-studied theologians. What I am trying to say is that if, like me, you avoid certain parts of God's Word like the plague, please ask Jesus to give you a fresh revelation of what *He* has to say to you. I truly believe you will be as surprised as I was.

Back to the lesson learned by this often reluctant student. I read the words that come before the "temple of the Holy Spirit" text, which say:

> *"I have the right to do anything," you say—but not everything is beneficial. "I have the right to do anything"—but I will not be mastered by anything. You say, "Food for the stomach and the stomach for food, and God will destroy them both." The body, however, is not meant for sexual immorality but for the Lord, and the Lord for the body* (1 Cor. 6:12–13).

This passage is about sexual immorality, but Jesus used it to speak to me about my relationship with food. In a listening prayer conversation, I sensed Him give me three simple questions to ask myself about my relationship with food. If you have a similar struggle as mine, or a different kind of struggle with food or body image, I pray that asking yourself these questions will take you toward wholeness as well.

1. If I have made all food permissible for you, then are you choosing to eat what is good for you?

In my case, sadly not always. I have both over-eaten and under-eaten. I am the queen of diets. I have undergone the torture of the most popular diet plans: liquid meal replacements, cabbage obsessions, and protein feasts alike. I've even offered myself up as a guinea pig for new diet drug trials. All failed. I know you have heard this before, but…diets don't work. The basic truth is that you need to burn off more calories than you consume. Simply put, eat less and move more.

2. Does what you want to eat have mastery over you?

Another way of phrasing this question is to say, "Can I say no to my soul and body when they want to eat that cream cake, bag of chips, or chocolate bar?" I have proclaimed that I am more than a conqueror at church on a Sunday morning, only to be defeated by apple crumble and cream that same afternoon! On a serious note, food addiction is just that—an addiction. In a way, it's one of the worst, although we hear about it much less than drug, alcohol, sex, and gambling addictions. Unlike other addictions, we can't simply give up the focus of our addiction; we have to eat food to survive. How great then is this simple question raised by Jesus?

3. "Food is for the stomach and the stomach for food." So what are you feeding—your body or your soul? Are you just filling a need, like frustration, anger, tiredness, or boredom with food?

I had eaten food for all of these reasons and more. If you know that you are eating for every reason other than satisfying your hunger, I gently suggest you seek emotional inner healing. The extensive and spiritually deep work of my South African friend Amanda Buys is a good place to start. You can access all her teaching free of charge on her Website.[1]

At the time of writing, I'm in the process of slowly losing weight. I currently weigh over 100 kilograms (220 pounds), so I'm not yet writing as one of those slimming club success stories (sorry to disappoint—but I don't have one of those pictures of me standing with both my legs inside one leg of a giant pair of trousers). I'll say as honestly as I can, I'm in a process, journeying along the path toward health. I often take two steps forward only to take one back, but onward I can only go, because I am being drawn, wooed, by God Himself. He's calling me forward, shouting encouragement along the way, and walking beside me.

Food, glorious food! The pleasure we gain just from enjoying a wonderful meal with family or friends can be life-affirming; but I believe there are boundaries that God puts around food and sex alike. Both are to be enjoyed, savored, and celebrated, but this enjoyment is a secondary blessing to its original purpose. God is the God of double blessing: sex was intended for the procreation of the human race, set within God's safe boundary, marriage; food was created for the sustenance of our physical bodies, set within the boundaries of a healthy balanced diet; and both have the secondary blessing of being highly enjoyable. Whenever we move outside the boundaries set by a loving God, though, we will eventually experience or cause pain. The pain we cause to ourselves or others can be likened to abuse. You were *not* created to be abused. Let me say that again. *You* were *not* created to be abused spiritually, emotionally, or physically. Let's make sure we recognize those facts.

We are all created equal yet different. I am not meant to look exactly like all other women. Many years ago a friend playfully made a comment about me: "Mandy, you are built for comfort and not for speed." I didn't take it as a slur—in fact, I have come to love his description of me, as I believe that (despite not being a Christian) he spoke prophetically into my life. And one Sunday that belief was confirmed.

As I've explained, I am a big woman. I am definitely the shape to toboggan rather than to ski.

Keith and I are members of what our home church[2] in Basel, Oikos, calls The Aaron Group. We are a diverse group of men and women who stand as spiritual mothers and fathers to the congregation and who support the leaders of our church, much as Aaron and Hur supported Moses' arms in Exodus 17:10–12.

One Sunday, our pastors Larwin and Silvia Nickelson were preaching on Malachi 4:6: "He will turn the hearts of the parents to their children and the hearts of the children to their parents...." All the young adults were invited to come to the front if they had issues with their parents and needed to be brought back into right relationship with them. As a spiritual mother in the Aaron group, I went forward to pray, to stand in for their actual parents who could not or would not be there. I randomly chose to stand in front of a beautiful young woman who had her eyes shut. In a quick prayer I asked God what this girl needed and what I should do. I sensed the Father wanted me to simply give her a hug. This is easy for me, as I love to hug and be hugged. As I held this young woman and prayed over her, she just dissolved into floods of tears. For the longest time I just held her close to me. It was only after the service had finished that we had time to talk about what she'd experienced. What she said was a revelation to me. She confessed that at first she was disappointed that it was a woman who had prayed for her.

She had issues with her father, and had asked God for a strong man of God to stand for her, in place of her dad. She said it was the first touch of my ample bosom that told her, to her disappointment, that God had sent her a woman and not a man. However, she went on to say that having a mother's embrace comforted her enough for her to just let go and let God deal with her pain.

As I said before, our God really is the God of double blessing. Not only did He comfort this young woman, but He used my size and womanliness as His means to do that. I learned a lot that day, and I began to thank Him for who I was, right there in that moment.

How do I view my body, his temple, now? I can tell you that the indwelling presence of the Holy Spirit is transforming me. Sometimes the process is frustratingly slow, but I continue to be encouraged by Jesus' words about my body. In another listening prayer session, I heard Him give this perspective: "Mandy, you have despised the body that I choose to inhabit by My Spirit. Don't you remember where I was born? A rough cave, a place where no one would intentionally choose to stay. I accommodated you by limiting My being to live as one of you, fully God living as fully human. Where I lived on earth was humble; where I live now in Heaven is glorious. My living in you is the same; from humble beginnings you'll be made, and are being made, into someone resembling My glory. I know it's difficult for you to grasp, but you will fully understand one day soon, when we meet face to face. I'm so looking forward to that Mandy...I can't wait. You'll see, soon my love, soon, very soon."

ENDNOTES

1. *Journey2Freedom* and *Healing our Wounded Hearts* by Amanda Buys, available at Kanaan Ministries; www.kanaanministries.org.

2. Oikos International Church; www.oikos-church.ch.

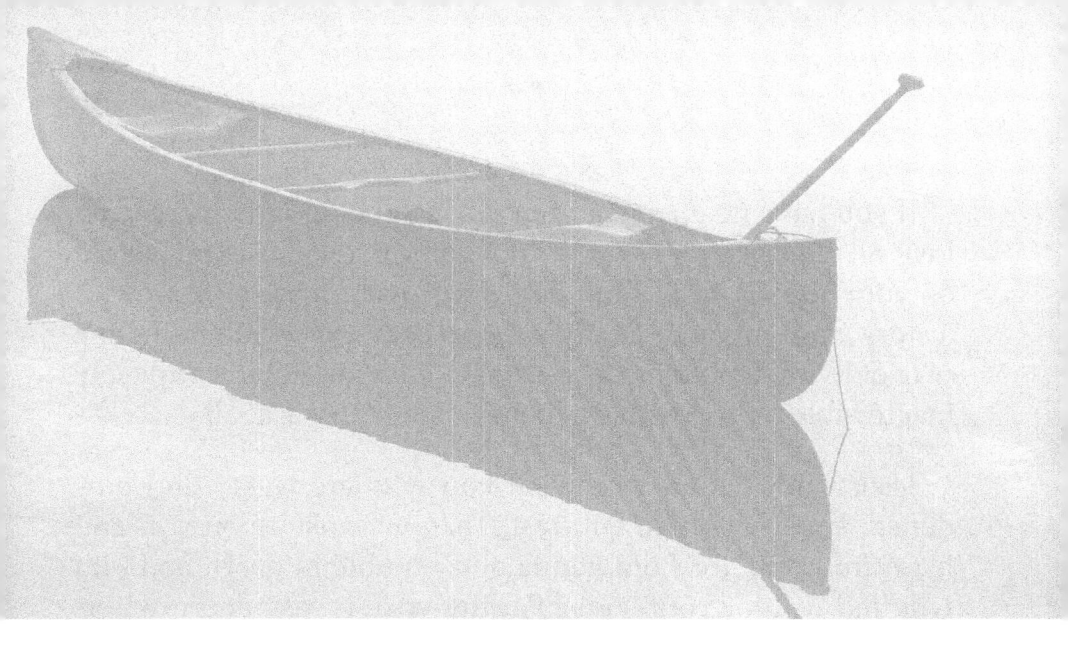

Chapter 7

To Be or Not to Be...

Women today all around the world are drowning in the turbulent waters of busyness. There are ever-increasing demands on mums to become some kind of superwomen—managing the home and the ceaseless activities of children, not to mention the millstone of expectation to look great all the time—and on over-stressed women in the workplace who have to strive just to get onto the corporate ladder, let alone fight their way up it. And the women who are doing both...my prayers are especially for you. I pray for all women, no matter what position you hold or title you define yourself by, that Jesus will reveal to you the vast chasm of difference between the desolate land of Doing and the tranquil shores of Being.

If you have no idea what I'm talking about, don't worry, my love, all will be made clear! I'm not going to put any extra weight on your already tired shoulders. I just want to show you, with a story from my own life, how Jesus draws us continually to a way of living that to most is so alien, it seems either completely inaccessible or impossible to believe that it exists at all.

Jesus said, "Come to me, all you who are weary and burdened, and I will give you rest. Take my yoke upon you and learn from me, for I am gentle and humble in heart, and you will find rest for your souls. For my yoke is easy and my burden is light" (Matt. 11:28–30).

These words may already be familiar to you, or you may have never heard them before. Take your time; re-read the words. Do you feel His personal invitation to you today? Does your soul long for this to become reality in your life—not just words that your mind agrees with, but a living reality in every area in your life?

I am an administrator at heart. I am an organizer too. I thrive on order and love to see a plan through to fruition. As a little girl I delighted in having a new stationery or pencil set to use, a rainbow of colored pencils lined up like soldiers awaiting their orders. My life before children involved working within the English Magisterial Courts system as a court administrator. I loved it. It was all formality and paperwork—a kind of Heaven on earth for me, if the truth be known.

In the 1990s the economic climate seemed to encourage everyone to be an entrepreneur. The world told us that the real money was to be made by working for yourself. So, with a girlfriend, I set up a small wedding business. By this time I'd had my first daughter, Georgia, and Keith was traveling all over England working for an IT software company and studying for an MBA in his spare time. What spare time? We just worked. Life wasn't lived for its own sake; we constantly strived for something better, that something better which we believed meant more…more money, more possessions, more influence.

Looking back on those times, I am so grateful that in meeting Jesus, another way opened up for me. Here was a life to really be lived, glorious, exciting, and full. In 1998 I met Jesus and began following Him as I've already described. After my conversion I was soon drawn into the life of the church. My skills were tailor-made for the role of church administrator. I worked for the five churches in the ecumenical partnership of West Swindon and the Lydiards, in the lovely county of Wiltshire. I loved my job. As a baby Christian, coming from no religious background, I had a lot to learn. I knew nothing of church life, and my learning curve was steep. Staff meetings were particularly interesting to me, and I kept interrupting the clergy team members to ask them why they did what they did. What did this or that mean? Did Jesus do these things, and if not, why did we have to do them?

I worked for a wonderful man named Andrew Hetherington, the rector whose wife, Sylvia, first invited me to church (as described in the first chapter). He is a gentle, humble man who really loves Jesus. He was the first person to begin teaching me about not doing, but being. Every summer the church ran a children's camp. As the administrator, I was heavily involved in its organization.

It's worth telling you more about myself at this point: I am a woman who, despite having two daughters of her own, is actually not that great when it comes to interacting with young children. I tell you this so you can understand my utter distress at the prospect of being responsible for one of the kids' groups at the camp. To be blunt, I hated it, really hated it, to the point of being distraught at the thought of a whole week of perceived torture.

My boss approached me at the end of the first day. I was sure he was going to reprimand me for my lack of enthusiasm with the children. Instead, he simply asked, "What are you still doing here, Mandy?"

I felt a little flustered and mumbled something like, "I thought I had to be here."

He broke out in a huge smile that disconcerted me further, and started to laugh. "No, Mandy, you're not expected to do everything!"

My relief must have been written all over my face. "I'm so sorry," I said, "it's just not me."

He looked me in the eyes with a very serious expression and said, "From this day onward Mandy, you are excused from working in the children's ministry."

"Really?" I said, "I mean, really? Is that OK? Is that acceptable?"

Why do we have such a narrow view of our worth, as if we have to excel at everything to be accepted? This, right here, is the difference between doing and being. I was doing what I thought I should—what I felt duty-bound to do. I was walking the path of man-made religious expectation, rather than God's ordained way. He has put in me, as He has every other human being, His way to "be," using the gifts given to us individually before we were even born. I know the phrase is over-used but I'll say it anyway: we are human *beings,* not human *doings.*

As the years passed, I stumbled across my way of discovering what God has put inside me. I've made mistakes while pursuing who I am in Jesus, but God still loves me, despite my mistakes. As we learn more about ourselves, God wants to partner with us more in His work. He doesn't wait until we are perfected before He deems us fit to join His great tapestry of history.

In 2001 we moved our family to Basel in Switzerland, since the company Keith worked for was moving its headquarters. We made our home in Switzerland and have now been here for over twelve years. We knew that God was using Keith's work to bring us to Switzerland, and we soon began to work with God. We started to run Alpha courses for English speaking expats (expatriates: people who have left their own country to live in another, usually for an extended period). We started small, with courses running twice a year in our own home. God was with us; the courses grew too big for our home, and we moved it into a church in Basel that allowed us to use their facilities.

We worked together with a wonderful group of Christians made up from different denominations, all of whom have become dear friends. Keith and I were seen as the mum and dad of the group. We led our little team and had a lot of fun with God on the way. For me, even though I was sharing the leadership with Keith, my role was in the kitchen cooking and doing the administration behind the scenes. Both were skills that I have, but I longed to stand by Keith's side at the front and interact more with the guests. As the years went by, I began to despise the role I had joyfully and willingly embraced at the start. I was quietly critical of others, because I felt I was doing all the hard work while my friends were enjoying themselves. This left me feeling bitter and frustrated.

We finished our spring Alpha courses just before Easter. Keith and I are leaders of what our church calls "Shabbat" (Sabbath) groups, which meet on Friday nights, just as Jesus would have done. We eat together, take communion, and bless one another. It was at our celebration of Passover that God gave to Keith individual words for each member of our group. He went around blessing each one with a message from the Father. He left me until last, hesitating before he gave the word for me. I remember that he first said, "Mandy, this word is meant as an encouragement." So then, through my husband, God said to me, "What good is it for someone to gain the whole world, and yet forfeit their very self?" (Luke 9:25).

I was not happy, to say the least. My poor husband just looked sheepishly at me and said, "They're not my words…it's what God gave me for you. It's to encourage you!"

We didn't discuss it further, but those words stayed with me all summer, just hanging in the air, waiting for me to acknowledge them, ask the Father about them, and be changed by them. I knew deep in my spirit that God was challenging my attitude to working on Alpha. I had nurtured a martyr spirit which, left unchecked, would destroy me. Instead of humbly agreeing with the Father, I chose to ignore His not-so-gentle prompting to stop my involvement in Alpha. In short, I ignored Him and His advice, spiritualizing it away. I came to the autumn having convinced myself that I was to go the extra mile and overcome my difficulties with Alpha.

The autumn course was prepared with just as much care and prayers as ever. The course took place, and through it, people came to faith in Jesus. However, for me it was awful. I was truly miserable. What began all those years ago with enjoyment, satisfaction, and peace became work, work, work with no reward of joy. I struggled every week. I became increasingly angry due to my false perception that no one was helping me, and this showed in my interaction with the team. My unhappiness found expression through a lack of attentiveness instead of my usual fastidious organization. I knew I had allowed myself to become slap-dash (sloppy), but I didn't care. To put it plainly, I was a grumpy old cow and not a joy to be around. In truth, I was tired, and by the end of the course I was at my wit's end. One evening I turned to Keith and told him I couldn't carry on anymore. I had had enough.

Keith's reply to me was, "Finally!" He went on to say that since I was ignoring what God had to say to me, he, Keith, had no chance of being listened to either. So he had left the matter with the Holy Spirit for Him to deal with.

I had come to my end. There was nothing left in me to give. I had to accept that what God had spoken to me earlier in the year was what must happen. I was humbled and repented of my pride and need for control. I had begun well by being, only to fall headlong into the pit of doing everything in my own strength. I was on my face, in the mud of my own making. Yet the Father didn't leave me there. He gently lifted me up and invited me to stop and rest. Stop and rest. Stop and rest.

I kept mulling the words over in my mind. What did stop and rest mean? OK, by stepping down from my leadership role in Alpha I was stopping, but I sensed that stopping was much more than that. I was restless at home. I still did my daily Bible reading and journaling but I couldn't stay still. I was so tired, just like a little baby who longs to feed but fusses and can't settle on the mother's breast. It took months of inactivity to even begin the process of stopping. I was like an oil tanker on the ocean: the captain may push the stop button at the helm, but it takes miles to come to a complete halt. My Christian identity was so bound up in the Alpha course: I had met Jesus on the course, and worked on it in both England and Switzerland. I really didn't know how to be myself outside of Alpha.

After about six months, my thoughts began to turn to the issue of resting. What was this? I knew it wasn't putting my feet up on the sofa and watching daytime TV. There was a deeper pool to be discovered, but I had no clue where to start looking for it. I asked God about it but He was quiet, just as He wanted me to be quiet. We had invited a dear friend to dinner one evening, Dave Olson, our spiritual dad and mentor. I had an ulterior motive in my invitation. Dave has an especially close relationship with Jesus, and I knew if anyone knew what rest was, he would. So after an unusually hurried supper I got right to the point. Handing Dave a cup of coffee I came right out and asked him.

"So, Dave," I said. "What do I have to do to rest?"

He sat impassively on the sofa enjoying his drink. *He couldn't have heard me,* I thought, so I repeated my question, this time with a little more vigor. "Dave, what do I have to DO to rest?" There was a pause, a broad smile and then he started to laugh—really laugh. I couldn't believe it. Did he think I was joking?

"No, really, Dave, WHAT DO I DO?"

He looked at me with the kindness of Jesus in his eyes and said simply, "Mandy, you don't DO anything!"

I am glad to say that over the next six months Jesus did begin my teaching in the area of resting. He used this classic piece of Scripture to bring me to rest.

A psalm of David

> *The LORD is my shepherd, I lack nothing. He makes me lie down in green pastures, he leads me beside quiet waters, he refreshes my soul. He guides me along the right paths for his name's sake. Even though I walk through the darkest valley, I will fear no evil, for you are with me; your rod and your staff, they comfort me.*
>
> *You prepare a table before me in the presence of my enemies. You anoint my head with oil; my cup overflows. Surely your goodness and love will follow me all the days of my life, and I will dwell in the house of the LORD forever* (Psalm 23).

I want to encourage you that learning to live a lifestyle of rest is not always easy, but it is liberating. If you think you are excluded from this wondrous place called rest due to the necessity of earning a living, listen up. Learning to rest starts with a change of heart attitude; this in turn will lead to a change in your thinking. Rest in its essence is not about inactivity but more about relying on God rather than your own abilities.

So, whether the majority of your life is spent in the work place or at home—or as more often than not, a dizzying mix of the two—you too can take hold of and truly thrive in this newfound place. It will also enable you to operate in your gifting. Resting in the arms of Jesus is the answer to being truly yourself.

It has taken some time of knowing Jesus to understand many of the wonderful things He has put in me—the Father's gifts. Abba destined me to have certain gifts that would be part of what Mandy is to become.

If you would like to discover more about what the Father has already put within you, there are many spiritual exercises you can do. Kanaan Ministries[1] has excellent teaching on the redemptive gifts of God. You might like to take the test that Kanaan Ministries provides and have the Father delight in showing you how He has created you to function in rest, in being.

So just before I move on, I want to be honest with you. I'm on my way. I have boarded the boat toward the land of Being. I have definitely left the land of Doing, but the strength of its influence does sometimes affect the currents of the sea of life on which I sail. I have to ask that the wind of the Holy Spirit fill my sails and direct me closer to the shore of Being and that I can anchor myself in the bay of rest itself, Jesus; the bay that enfolds my little boat like the arms of a mother who draws her child to her breast. In the next chapter I share with you some of the things I have been learning.

Endnote

1. *Man's Purpose and the Gifts of the Spirit, Book 1 of Journey2Freedom* by Amanda Buys, available at Kanaan Ministries; www.kanaanministries.org.

Chapter 8

Stop and Smell the Roses

In the previous chapter I described how Jesus led me to stop, and in that stopping I started to discover the reality of rest. It's in this harbor of rest that we learn what it is to *be*.

Be Present

As a child, I was extraordinarily self-controlled and ordered. Everything in my life had its place. My bedroom was freakily tidy—according to my mum it was tidier than the rest of the house. (This was not typical childhood behavior, I've since discovered, with two daughters leaving trails of their presence all over the place.) And as an adult I've lived most of my life in the future tense. I was always preparing myself for life's "what ifs," my mind racing ahead to control events that hadn't even happened yet.

To say that I planned the birth of our first daughter, Georgia, would be an understatement. I had even put corned beef sandwiches in our freezer in preparation for the trip to hospital. You might wonder what on earth sandwiches have got to do with childbirth, but I had read so much about getting the birth checklist right, that I even followed the advice about making a snack for your husband, just in case you experience a long labor. Guess what—my preparedness was rewarded. My labor was 26 hours long and Keith did indeed eat my lovingly prepared offering—much to my revulsion at the time, as he leaned over to me mid-contraction kindly offering to share his lunch. (Meanwhile the radio in our room serenaded me with a track by Salt and Pepper, "Let's Talk about Sex Baby." As you can imagine, corned beef sandwiches and sex were the last things on my mind!)

Jesus has since shown me that much of my control was born out of a need to be self-reliant, a trait of someone who has an "orphan spirit." Those who have an orphan spirit feel alone and abandoned, and therefore think they have to sort everything out for themselves. I've also learned that control is the flip-side, or distortion, of my genuine God-given gift of authority and leadership.

God has many names in the Bible. In Hebrew, the name El Shaddai is one of my favorites and translated generally means "The Almighty, all-sufficient God." Other Judaic translations refer to this name as the "many-breasted one." It sounds strange, doesn't it? A bit like a Hindu god. But I have experienced this El Shaddai love and comfort. Genesis 49:25 says, "because of your father's God, who helps you, because of the Almighty, who blesses you with blessings of the skies above, blessings of the deep springs below, blessings of the breast and womb." How comforting. Just as when a baby is on the breast, she is at rest; she is dependent; she is intimately and naturally just *being present*. No worries, no future events to organize, no expectation to be anything other than in the here and now of her mother's breast.

Unlike this picture of a contented child, I've come to realize that I've wasted so much of my life living in a dimension that was not reality. As a young mother I continually looked forward: the first smile, first steps, and the first day at school. Before I knew it, my girls were young women. Where did their childhoods go? Where was I that I missed so much? But now God is helping me in my gradual discovery of what it means to be truly present in every moment.

The art of *being* isn't a secret only known to mystics. It is entered into by the process of stopping and resting. How long it takes to get there is different for each of us. Some can access this state with relative ease. For most, I suspect, like me, it takes much longer—perhaps even a lifetime—but we are not alone in this process. We can have a constant companion. The Holy Spirit is not only our Comforter, He is our guide too. He is our Enabler and gives us power to live this life, the power that is available through Jesus living in us by His Spirit.

Our God is a God with a great sense of humor, and the chosen vessel of His message just to *be* came to me in the form of a shaggy dog. When Benson, our brown and white bearded collie, entered the Muckett household like a little whirlwind of excited friendliness, I was transported right back to being a new mum again. No longer did I have all the time in the world to do what I wanted. I couldn't turn him off when I felt like it and store him in a cupboard until the time that I deemed fit for organized play or a walk. No, he dragged me, literally dragged me, back into the present. It's as if I woke up from a deep sleep the moment he arrived; this sleeping beauty is now fully awake. Our crazy, adorable dog has not only stolen the hearts of our family, he has me actually stopping to smell the roses that adorn the hedges on our many walks.

I am connecting with Keith at a new level too. Walking in the local vineyards with the one you love (Keith, that is) is not only romantic, it is also a spiritual classroom. From scrambling through weeds and stumbling on rocky paths to seeing what happens to trailing vines, God has used many of our dog walks to teach me precious lessons.

I don't know what Jesus will have stored up for you on your journey, or whether it will come via a shaggy dog, but He, by His Spirit, will enable and empower you to live a life of being. And He will not be content until He has you in this place.

BE SURRENDERED

There is an internationally recognized gesture for surrender: both arms raised in the air. I find this fascinating, as it's also a posture of worship: raising holy hands. Yet surrender has such negative connotations. In warfare it means to give up, to be defeated. The world today does not have many positive things to say about surrender. Everyone is encouraged to live their lives, as Frank Sinatra aptly sang, "My Way," but what does Jesus say about surrender? This is what I've learned so far.

Jesus is the epitome of surrender. He gave Himself up completely for us even unto death, but He was not defeated; He was resurrected. Of all the figures in all of the world's religions, only He is *still alive.*

For me there are three levels of surrender that Jesus has gently led me into so far. The first is the most obvious and in some respects the easiest—the surrender of holding on to all of the rubbish in my life. When I gave my life to Jesus I left all of that stuff at the foot of His cross. It took some time to surrender, or let go of it, but with His help, I did. Jesus took on Himself everything I did, thought, or said that separated me from God, and paid the price I should pay.

The second surrender, which is a daily choice, is that of my will—choosing to believe that it's just possible that an all-powerful, all-knowing, ever-present God might, just might, have a better plan for me than I could ever have for myself. Mary, the mother of Jesus, humbly chose to surrender to Gods' will: "'I am the Lord's servant,' Mary answered. 'May your word to me be fulfilled.' Then the angel left her" (Luke 1:38).

Jesus teaches us by His own example in the garden of Gethsemane; just before He was betrayed, He surrendered His will to God:

> *Going a little farther, he fell with his face to the ground and prayed, "My Father, if it is possible, may this cup be taken from me. Yet not as I will, but as you will"* (Matthew 26:39).

Jesus was enabled to let go of what He wanted because of His deep, loving, trusting relationship with His Father. We too can access this ability to trust, through Jesus Himself, by His Spirit. This process is ongoing, so I ask Jesus what He thinks about situations that present themselves in my life. It's not so much the old wristband slogan WWJD: What Would Jesus Do? as What do You think and feel about my situation, Jesus? Give it a try—you might be transformed by what He says to you.

The third lesson I'm currently learning about surrender is, for me and I imagine most people, a little difficult to understand. I believe that God sometimes also asks us to surrender our dreams to Him as well. That may seem a strange concept as it's often God who gives us our dreams and desires in the first place. I have had a promise from the Lord about my body's health and size. His words to me were, "I will do it. Let Me do it." I have held on to this promise over the years, still believing despite the number on the bathroom scales. My favorite verse in the Bible is, "Blessed is she who believes that what the Lord has said to her shall be accomplished" (Luke 1:45). However, Jesus has asked if I would surrender even this good thing to Him. Would I surrender—let go of—this desire, even if it meant that my size and shape remained the same for the rest of my life? It was a challenge because my desire is obviously a good one; to be slimmer would be good for my general health as well as boosting my self-esteem. I am still a little perplexed by it, but I believe He uses this type of surrender for His greater purposes.

At the time of writing these words I am attending a women's conference in the United States. The following verse really spoke to me:

But God chose the foolish things of the world to shame the wise; God chose the weak things of the world to shame the strong (1 Corinthians 1:27).

Could it be that God would choose a big girl with a "special eye" to encourage women about their intrinsic and irreplaceable beauty? Could it be that even my greatest desires are blocking the "more" that God actually has to bestow on me? These are still questions I am pondering, with the help of Jesus' Spirit. I'll let you know how I get on—I'm in a process too, don't forget. I'm not perfect. As Joyce Meyers has said, "Many people feel that God can't use them because they're not perfect—this is a lie. God (the Potter) uses cracked pots (that's us) to do His work."[1] And I'm just like a cracked pot, with Jesus' light shining out into a dark world through my imperfections.

BE CONTENT

What does *content* mean? For the longest time I had completely the wrong interpretation of this word in my life's dictionary. To me, contentment meant making do with second best, or accepting not having enough. I know I'm not the only one who misunderstood this word. We struggle to find contentment, but still feel guilty that we want more. Like Oliver Twist we cry out, "Can I have some more?" Women today are actually actively encouraged to want more, to have it all, so to speak, but it is a more that is destructive, self-centered, and which ultimately leads us away from Jesus.

The world tells women not to be content, but to constantly improve ourselves, especially our bodies. The boom in cosmetic surgery is testament to this fact. Now it is not my intention to sling the mud of judgment in your face. I do have my opinions about cosmetic surgery. I have decided what I won't do to my body. I am learning to love myself as I am right now, as I already live with the consequences of my bad decisions about food consumption. The world will tell us to maintain our youth for as long as is humanly possible. My questions to myself and to you are, "Is what is 'humanly possible' good for me? Is it what God wants for me? Is this God's ordained way?" These are huge questions, and you will only get the answers from the Father Himself. I believe the medical profession has much to bless us with, but there's a massive difference between a breast reduction to help with crippling back pain or a modest enlargement that is appropriate if a chest is as flat as the proverbial pancake—and the type of procedures that distort a woman's body. I'm thinking of the current fashion for pumped up lips and boobs and faces that no longer can express any emotion. Come to God the Father and ask Him what He thinks. I believe we would all make different decisions if we asked Him about it first!

As I've said, I'm not standing in judgment over the surgery you may have already had or are considering—I'm looking into having cosmetic surgery myself. I'm partially sighted, with only 20 percent vision in my right eye. My childhood was colored by many visits to an eye hospital. I suffered name-calling by local kids because I had to wear a patch with my pink NHS glasses. My sight has never improved, and the operation I had as a child to straighten the muscle that moves the eye has weakened it to the point that I now have one of those "special eyes" that can see in the opposite direction of my good eye. I can joke about it now because Jesus has healed the shame I suffered. I can look in a mirror now and see beauty, not a beast. That's OK; if Jesus accepts me just the way I am, then I guess I can accept myself too.

Yes, He loves us as we are right now, but He has so much more for us. At first I religiously disregarded the prompting to consider eye surgery, believing I was not actually hearing Jesus but just my soul's desire, considering it frivolous and a move toward vanity—but after I got over myself, I chose to believe Jesus might have another opinion about it: perhaps it's a gift He wants to give me. His gifts are perfect; they are not tainted like gifts of the world. So by the time you read my words I may well have my special eye in check. Whatever happens, I long to remain in step with His plan for my life, to do His good and perfect will.

What I suggest for you is that you ask Jesus before you leap into what, in His opinion, could be unnecessary for you. Many people have undergone the knife, had tattoos or body piercing, only to find that once their scars are healed, they still feel incomplete, and their souls still cry out for more. If you are one of these women who are silently screaming for more, cry out to Jesus—He will be the more you crave and you will find peace for your soul. For the source of our contentment is found in Him and Him alone. It is through resting and being in Him that we can take hold of contentment in every area of our lives. I see the contentment Jesus offers as loving acceptance and gratitude. Do you want to live this? I do! It is a life that, despite not being perfect, is a place of peace and satisfaction. No more striving, no more keeping up with the Joneses. (Who are those Joneses anyway?)

BE APPRECIATIVE

It is our damaged human nature to compare ourselves with others—our circumstances, our bodies, our abilities. We are constantly comparing everything, making judgments for or against, judgments that we pass down to others from our own little gods.

Women are especially affected by the blight of personal comparison. My little sister Carol likes the smell of lilies. Can you believe that? I think they smell terrible. Our opinions don't affect the lily itself—it is able to just be what God created it to be, a beautiful flower—but our preferences can affect others. We women are guilty of abusing other women by the treatment we inflict on their flower's delicate soul. By constantly comparing ourselves with others, we can also unwittingly damage ourselves. We fall into two opposite temptations. We can become proud and self-elevating when we consider ourselves better than someone else, or we beat up our own souls when we believe we are less in comparison. Have you ever heard a gardener call a flower ugly? No, never. A flower is a flower. Flowers by their very nature are beautiful. *Beautiful.*

Just as we prefer some flowers to others, we prefer the company of some women to others. It's OK to invest in friendships, but not to shun the women we don't relate to, to overlook them, or even intentionally avoid them. It's not like that in the Garden Heart of God. Yes, He may group certain types of flowers together in His borders, but He has a special place for each individual flower, which only that flower can fill. If you've felt isolated by others who haven't appreciated your unique qualities, don't worry. The Father Gardener has special treatment in store for you. He sees and appreciates your beauty. He will open the others' eyes as well one day; just rest in His individual love for you. His love will sustain you and His grace will carry you to that day when your bloom will be recognized.

For those of us who are guilty of either comparing other women or ourselves, loving forgiveness is freely and immediately available to us when we confess what we have done. Speak to Jesus; bring your self-righteous judgments to His cross, and He will not only give you His forgiveness, He can and will open your eyes to see the beauty of God's Garden Heart. You will see the beauty that lives in you and the women all around you. Go on, I dare you to do something I love doing. Go up to a woman you don't know and tell her she's beautiful. You won't be hauled off in a strait jacket, I promise. You might be met with suspicion at first, but tell her that God sees her beauty. For those who are shy, your challenge might be to start with someone you know first—not so scary. Go on, I dare you—you'll love the responses you get, and you will bless women in so doing.

If you are learning to be present, content, and appreciative, you are well on your way to a life of being, a life lived out of rest; you are learning to stop and smell the roses. There is another question to ask, though: What kind of fragrance, or influence, are *you*?

BE FRAGRANT

Perfume plays a part in the story of many women. Whether we wear it or not, fragrance is one of those memory makers. The fragrance of our girlfriends, mothers, or grandmothers, when remembered, replays the tapes of our lives. My mother is known for her favorite perfume, a strong, spicy scent that hangs in the air long after it's sprayed. Mum loved it so much when I was a child that she would drench herself in it. At times it was a little overwhelming, in a good way, of course, like my mum herself (love you Mum). If the perfume bottle came out, you knew you were going to get some of it too. I guess that's a good picture of how my mother influenced my life. Her fragrance touched me, and still does to this day.

Like an expensive perfume, the essence of a woman was made to linger. The Father Gardener has created in each of us an individual scent, one that no one else has. In fact it is so individual that it cannot be replicated. It cannot be manufactured. It belongs only to you. It has your name on the bottle. It is made from your flower. It is made by Him for you. We were created to have an influence in our world:

> *But thanks be to God, who always leads us as captives in Christ's triumphal procession and uses us to spread the aroma of the knowledge of him everywhere. For we are to God the pleasing aroma of Christ among those who are being saved and those who are perishing* (2 Corinthians 2:14-15).

Our beauty is to reflect the beauty of Jesus: a lasting beauty that speaks of the Father's love and draws people to know that love. Do you want your life to be a love that lingers, a life filled with an aroma that influences? Or, like a little girl determined to smash her mum's rose petals into homemade perfume, are your impurities and selfish desires creating a less attractive aroma that doesn't last?

There are many ways to fall short of God's intended, lingering fragrance for our lives. Some of us are like artificial flowers, which have no scent at all. We have created a false, outward appearance of perfection, a life hidden behind a facade. The fear is, however, that one day soon we will be discovered. Our life may be exposed for the sham it is. We cling to the artificial even though there's no life or joy to it—nothing that has the ability to linger. If you identify with these artificial flowers, there is hope for you. Our Gardener God has sent His Son to you to offer you His real, authentic life. It's a life not just to be lived, but lived with exuberance. As John 10:10 says, "I [Jesus] have come that they may have life, and have it to the full."

Do you remember the 1980s fashion for dried flower arrangements and potpourri? You'd come into a room and be slapped in the face by a wall of floral essences. Some of us are like these dried flowers—once fresh flowers, but long since dead. They were often dyed shockingly bright colors and sprayed with concentrated oils in an attempt to recreate their former beauty. They create an atmosphere of a musty Victorian museum; these flowers only whisper of their long lost beauty. If this feels like you—faded, dusty, a museum piece—the Gardener God sent His Son so that your life can be resurrected. Jesus can give you a life that is naturally bright, fragrant, and can never be extinguished.

And some of us are like cut flowers. The ones I buy seem to last such a short time. Before I know, it they are wilting or turning brown; they don't linger. The reason for this, of course, is that they are already dying when I buy them. They are cut from their source of sustenance, only maintained for a little while in the small pool of water held by a vase. The first ever flower, Eve, was rooted in the Garden Heart of God. She was cared for, provided for, and nurtured by God Himself, but by believing a lie, her flower was cut from its Source.

Is your flower cut off from its Source? If you know that you are cut off from God, don't despair, beautiful one. Our Gardener God sent His Son just to reconnect you to the Source of life. You can connect right now wherever you are or whatever you are doing. So come, my lovely, whether you have been enduring a fake version of life, if your life died long ago with only an exhibit of it preserved on show for people to see, or if in fact you now know you have always been cut off from the Gardener's love—let's not waste any more of your precious life. With an open heart and a humble spirit, come back to the Father Gardener by accepting the free gift of eternal life through His Son, Jesus.

BE COLORFUL

Women come in all shapes and sizes—large, small, short, and tall, with varying shades of skin, hair, and eye color—and that's even before you get to how we choose to dress. What do I mean when I say "Be colorful"? Well it's more than just our race, our culture, or even our personality. *Being colorful* is in essence just being yourself, without compromise! Compromise is a fact of life, and we are all affected by it to one degree or other, but does God ask us to compromise who we really are for the sake of fitting in or being acceptable to others? Certainly not! In fact in Matthew 5:13–16, Jesus called His followers to be "salt and light." This means being who God created us to be, contrasting with and even bringing change to our surroundings—not just blending in.

Having moved frequently following Keith's career, I have had the opportunity to make many friends. Other than my close family, church, and old school friends, I am fortunate to have many girlfriends. I've made connections with women for various reasons, whether through work, children, or shared interests, and I have been blessed by knowing these women. However, there have also been times when these friendships have caused me pain. As I mentioned in a previous chapter, being a Christian isn't always easy in a world where anything goes and truth is relative. Having faith in Jesus and living a life pleasing to Him is a challenge. It is a challenge I became keenly aware of during a certain season of my life.

The shadow of compromise moved across my horizon so slowly I didn't notice it at first. I enjoyed time with my friends, chatting over coffee, sharing what was going on in our lives with mutual interest—until one particular afternoon. That day I came home feeling that I'd been completely left out of the conversation that revolved around activities and events I knew nothing about. I also knew that I'd been struggling for a long time with the challenge not to indulge myself with gossiping, and I knew this had set me apart somewhat, but something was still amiss. As the weeks went by I had a growing sense of being side-lined and even realized that I no longer was being invited to some functions. *Why was this?* I wondered. *Is it because I talk about Jesus too much?* I wrestled with these questions for a while and was discouraged because I enjoyed having the opportunity, where and when it arose, to share my faith. *Perhaps I should tone it down a bit,* I thought, *No one wants a Bible basher for a friend, right?* Still, I had a burning desire in me to tell women about Jesus.

As I mentioned near the beginning of this book, I hear God speaking to me in many ways, including through music. On one occasion I was listening to the car radio on my drive home. I was really low. You know the old saying, being lonely in a crowd? That was exactly how I felt. Although I'd spent time with others I was feeling isolated, but I wasn't sure how to deal with it. *If only I was more like them,* I thought, *perhaps they would like me more...perhaps I would fit in?* As soon as this question had drifted through my mind the song, "True Colors" by Cyndi Lauper[2] started to play, and it was as if God was singing the lyrics just to me, at that very moment. God used the words of this song to speak to me about my compromise between fitting in and truly just being myself. God used this song to encourage me that I was indeed beautiful just as I was, and that I shouldn't compromise who I truly am just for the sake of pleasing others.

Well I can tell you that my tears fell like the raindrops that make up the rainbow mentioned in the song—a rainbow that is created when God's light shines through our tears. Every word spoke of God's love for me, that He saw my struggles and my frustrations and that He was there for me—showing me my true worth. Since that day I've made every effort to stay true to who I am. Other people's perception of me is their issue, not mine. I am on a journey of self-acceptance because I know God loves me, and I choose every day to see myself through God's eyes.

Are you being true to yourself, or are you compromising who you really are in order to be like everyone else? God created your unique color, and you are essential to His palette of beauty. Why live a black and white existence trying to be like everyone else when you were made for His vivid, high definition, full color reality?

Go on; don't be ashamed of who you are—be colorful!

ENDNOTES

1. Taken from Joyce Meyer's audio teaching, "Key to Enjoying Every Single Day of Your Life"; the story

of the cracked pot. Available through www.joyce-meyer.org.

2. Cyndi Lauper, *True Colors,* words by Billy Steinberg and Tom Kelly, 1986 Portrait, Epic.

Chapter 9

"Life Is Like a Box of Chocolates..."

"Life is like a box of chocolates...you never know what you're gonna get," according to the unforgettable Forrest Gump, from the film of the same name. I do wonder, though, why Forrest didn't just read the little card you get in the box with those flowery descriptions of every chocolate in the box. How could he have missed that? It's part of the chocolate eating experience to take time to ponder the box of delights and choose your favorite.

Chocolate fills my memories of childhood, especially at Christmas. My family had its sweet treat traditions at Christmas time. For us, it was obligatory to have a huge, round, pink tin of Quality Street chocolates. (If you are English, you may have had a similar experience.) For me as a little girl, this pink tin contained jewels, real jewels, of all different shapes and colors, wrapped in shiny paper. It was a real privilege to be the first one to choose a sweet from the tin. My personal favorites were the chocolate-covered nuts, robed in royal purple. Next, I would choose anything with a caramel center, but never would I *ever* choose a strawberry cream. How disgusting! In fact, most of the chocolate creams were revolting. In our house these outcasts of the sweetie tin were left to fester. No who would ever eat them, not even as a last resort. I would have rather gone hungry, or horror of horrors, eat something healthy, like real fruit!

I'm reminded of a recent TV ad for a certain confection, a variety of chocolate-covered offerings like peanut, toffee, and biscuit. Lurking under some of the chocolate coats are the dreaded creams. In the advertisement, two men play Russian roulette; instead of guns to their temples they have to choose from this packet of chocolates. The first makes his choice. Relief sweeps his face, he chose well, a peanut. The second man chooses. Yes, toffee! The pressure is building. The first man chooses again—biscuit this time, phew. The second man's brow is now sprinkled with sweat. He chooses... Oh no, it's a coffee cream! Game over. The first man wins. (However, the second man smiles at the camera and says, "I like coffee!")

Please forgive my foray into chocolate nostalgia, but I do have a point to make. You see, Forrest Gump was actually speaking a deep truth. Our lives are like his box of chocolates, the one without the description card. No matter how we would love to choose what we experience in our lives, we can't. Our futures are unknown to us, and just like Forrest, we don't always know what we're going to get. This is the point I want to make. We would love it if all of our life's experiences were laid out on a card in front of us, written with all the details, so we could choose what we wanted and disregard the rest. Whoever heard of anyone choosing an awful life event willingly? Well, I know one man who has—Jesus. He chose an end that was utterly distasteful, and not even for His own sake, but because it was His Father's will. He chose to die on a cross for love's sake, for our sakes.

Life is a mystery, and because of this we all try to take control of our futures. We mostly try to make decisions that are good and that will benefit us. A few make decisions that will also benefit others, but basically we all cling to the known, taking hold of the most comfortable choices. But what if God is drawing us, even planning for us, to pick the strawberry creams of life? What do we think of God then? And will we, like Jesus, choose to do the Father's will, even when we don't know what the outcome will be? I'm challenging you (and myself) with one of the most basic yet important questions we have to answer: Will you trust God?

I was impacted as a very new Christian by reading *Hinds' Feet in High Places* by Hannah Hurnard,[1] a Christian classic. For those of you who haven't read it (and I highly recommend that you do), the story centers on Little Much Afraid, a young woman who takes a journey with the Shepherd to the high places. She is given two companions for the journey by the Shepherd Himself. Their names are Sorrow and Suffering—not the companions I would choose for a life journey. (They would have been called Strawberry and Orange Cream if they were in my life box of chocolates.) Little Much Afraid travels far and wide, experiencing great difficulty on the way. She is even led into a desert. The desert is used as a metaphor in a similar way in the Bible: a place of desolation and loneliness, where loss and emptiness are experienced. A place where none of us would choose to go voluntarily, yet somewhere we are all compelled to travel through at some point in our lives. It is a place that, more often than not, the Lord actually leads us to. We cry out in desperation for release from this awful place, where we believe nothing can survive, but look at what the Lord says:

> *Therefore I am now going to allure her; I will lead her into the wilderness and speak tenderly to her* (Hosea 2:14).

God always has purposes that, even if we discover some level of meaning to them, are high above and beyond what we can understand. They are more perfect than we can conceive, more loving than we can imagine, and so comprehensive that eternity itself cannot contain them. These next words voice this, in ways we can grasp:

> *"For I know the plans I have for you," declares the LORD, "plans to prosper you and not to harm you, plans to give you hope and a future"* (Jeremiah 29:11).

In the desert, as Little Much Afraid discovered, a tiny flower grows; this tiny little flower has a name. It is called Acceptance. Acceptance is a Yes, an Amen. We don't have to understand our difficult situations in order to humbly accept that this is where God has put us. He most often isn't the cause of our hardships, but He allows them because He is the only one who can use these things to draw us closer to Him, and make us so much more than we would ever be if we were left to our own devices. The devil may plan our deaths in the desert, but God plans life, and not just life, but abundant life. I'll quote it again:

> *The thief comes only to steal and kill and destroy; I have come that they may have life, and have it to the full* (John 10:10).

I'd like to tell you a story about this from my own life, a situation that I'm not sure I would have chosen had I known beforehand what it would entail. I've written in an earlier chapter about my birth father and stepdad, and the father issues I needed to deal with. Additionally, our church had been looking at Malachi 4:6, "He will turn the hearts of the parents to their children, and the hearts of the children to their parents." At the same time I'd been challenged in my daily prayer time with Jesus. He was reminding me of the fifth commandment, "Honor your father and your mother, so that you may live long in the land the Lord your God is giving you" (Exod. 20:12), particularly with regard to my birth father, Bob. Notice that the commandment doesn't say honor your mother and father if they are good parents. It just says to honor them.

I had met Bob for the first time at the funeral of his own father—a difficult time to meet anyone, let alone your father. He had visited me once, but I had shunned his advances to try to become the father he'd never been. The problem was that I already had a dad, my stepdad, John, the man I loved as my dad, who adopted me and gave me his name. He was my dad and I didn't need another. I was very polite and thanked Bob for giving me life, but said that I couldn't give him what he wanted, a relationship with me as his daughter.

Years had passed, and now Jesus was on my case. He said, "Mandy, you let Me use you to help others with father issues, but you're not reconciled to your own father." So, to keep the story short, I decided I would contact my father, for Jesus' sake. I would honor my earthly father. I didn't know how I was to achieve this, but contacting him and asking to visit him would be a start. I didn't long for a relationship with him, for by now I had met Abba Father, but I knew it was the right thing to do. It was what Jesus wanted of me, what Abba wanted of me, and what only the Holy Spirit could enable me to do.

In May I telephoned Bob, and after the expected initial awkwardness, I asked the question, "Can I come and visit you?"

Bob lived in the north of England at the time and my trip would involve flying from Switzerland. He was a little shocked, but very open to the trip, so it was all arranged. I would travel with my family to visit during the holidays in October. It was agreed. I put the phone down and knew I had taken the first step of turning to my father.

It was the third week in July when I received the phone call from my stepsister. Bob worked as a night security man, and during his night shift he'd had a massive heart attack and died. I did what I could to give words of comfort to a woman I had only met once; to some extent I knew how she felt, because my stepdad had died some years before. Yet at the same time it was as if I was having some kind of out-of-body experience. It was like looking at my own reactions from somewhere outside myself, perhaps to protect myself from any emotional overload. It was weird, and something I do not want to experience ever again.

At the time of Bob's death, our church was teaching about healing the sick, casting out demons, and raising the dead—doing all those things Jesus said we would do:

Very truly I tell you, whoever believes in me will do the works I have been doing, and they will do even greater things than these, because I am going to the Father (John 14:12).

The timing was eerily apt because in the last week of July we usually travel to England for the New Wine Christian camp in the West Country. We brought forward our trip to attend Bob's funeral before the camp. I was confused to say the least, but took comfort that God could raise the dead. I began to think that He might use me to pray for Bob to be resurrected. You think that this sounds a bit mad—was it wishful thinking or my grief talking? And how could I grieve for someone I didn't even know?

So we traveled to the funeral. I paid my respects to my father's body. I did take my faltering faith in my hands and pray for him to be raised from the dead, but nothing happened. We then continued on our planned holiday at New Wine. It's a yearly retreat for us as a family (despite the English climate not being ideal for camping!). It's a spiritual refill—an extended time of hearing God, being taught more about Him and just generally giving more space for Him in our busy lives.

It was a week unlike any I have experienced. The Bible verse chosen for the weekly morning study was "Jesus wept" (John 11:35), the shortest, yet one of the deepest verses in the Bible. Please take a break to just read those two words again, aloud. It comes from the story of Mary and Martha's brother Lazarus, also a friend of Jesus, who was sick. The sisters sent word for Jesus to come, as He was only two miles away, but He didn't go immediately. Despite knowing that Lazarus would die, Jesus stayed where He was and told the disciples that He would resurrect Lazarus, although the disciples did not grasp what He was saying to them.

Lazarus was already in the grave four days before Jesus turned up. Both sisters voiced the same ache, "If you would have been here our brother would not have died." The rest of the story relates that Jesus does in fact raise Lazarus from the dead, but just before He does this, there is this succinct verse, "Jesus wept." Part of me understands that He was genuinely sharing in the sisters' grief, because Lazarus was also His friend, but the mystery is that He did this knowing what was to come. Why?

Throughout the week I was very conflicted within myself. Grief hung over me like a mantle, but I didn't know why or even who I was grieving for. I knew that I had lost something, and that was what I could accept as the focus of my grief. I could grieve the father Bob never was. As I struggled with my emotions on each day of the holiday, the Lord kept bringing person after person to Keith and I, needing counsel or comfort. Inside I was crying out to God, "What about me? Comfort me! What have You done to me? Why have You allowed this to happen? You were the one who led me to this place! Why?"

The most difficult thing was that the headline speaker of the week, Bill Johnson, and so many of the other leaders kept mentioning resurrection time and time again, session after session. I couldn't escape the word. I didn't know whether Bob had made any profession of even simple faith in Jesus. I couldn't know whether he would even be saved, to be resurrected on the day of the Lord. God was silent. Abba Father was silent. Nothing. I heard nothing then, and to date have heard no explanation of what happened.

"Life Is Like a Box of Chocolates..."

In October I did travel back to England again to honor my planned visit. It was an especially difficult time, but it was the completion of what I had set out to do. It would be easy to say by going to his funeral and later returning for the visit, that I had in fact honored my birth father and that God in His mercy and compassion for me, knowing the time of Bob's death, drew me to reconcile with him. Both of these things are true. Yet the specter of the unanswered question still remains, the genuine plea of one who is confused and longs to understand. Wouldn't I have preferred that Bob was still alive? Other people in the Bible may have asked the same question. Consider Job—wouldn't he have wanted to keep his original family even though he was given another one? Wouldn't Naomi have preferred that her husband and sons hadn't died, even though she received a grandchild? All these are real, heartfelt questions, and it is our human desire to know everything, yet I'm constantly reminded that we are not God! It is not my intention to attempt to answer here one of the most asked questions about human suffering. However, I do believe the answers to all of our questions are found in Jesus.

I am on the leadership team of the women's ministry in our church, the Saphira women's group. We meet once every six weeks or so, and God always speaks to us as we wait on Him. It was at one of our meetings, while this book was in the editing stages, that Jesus spoke into my sadness and unanswered questions surrounding the time of my birth father's death. Fortunately our great friend Dave Olson was visiting from the States, and he was especially asked to speak at the meeting about God as Father.

Interestingly, Dave did not spend all night telling us about the differences between our earthly father and heavenly Father.

Instead he told us the story of two very painful moments in his life. The first was when he was asked to resign from the church of which he was pastor. In one devastating moment he lost his job, income, house, ministry, and reputation. Second, and most tragically, was the death of his first wife, Linda, who had fought and lost the battle with cancer. Dave poured out his heart to this room full of women, and silence held us captive as we listened to one person's struggle to understand the big question: Why? Dave recounted those awful times when God was silent, when He just seemed to have disappeared. There was seemingly a spiritual void with no answers, no comfort, nothing—just pain and then more pain.

I could really relate to how Dave had felt at these times. Yes, I echoed in my heart: Where were You, Lord? The strange thing was that Dave then started to speak about how he learned about the assurance of God, about His love and presence even in the darkest times of life. *Assurance? That can't be right,* I thought to myself. Yet Dave exuded such a firm and peaceful confidence. It was at this moment that the tears started to flow down my cheeks. The Holy Spirit nudged my memory about something the Lord had said to me many years ago, as Jesus had said He would, "But the Advocate [Counselor], the Holy Spirit, whom the Father will send in my name, will teach you all things and will remind you of everything I have said to you" (John 14:26).

Early in our walk with Jesus, Keith and I had attended a youth event in England called Cross Rhythms, a weekend Christian music festival held under canvas. We were a little old to be classed as youth but were eager to experience more contemporary worship music than we were used to in our local church. During the afternoons there were seminars on various subjects. After one of these seminars Keith asked for prayer from the speaker, Chris Coles, and it emerged during this prayer time that (unknown to me) Keith had put me on some kind of pedestal. His worship was directed at me instead of Jesus. I was surprised to hear Keith say this to Chris, but I was eager for him to be closer to Jesus. In a symbolic act, Keith gave me up to God, so that he could put Jesus where He belonged in his life—in first place. As Keith spoke out these words of renunciation, the Holy Spirit filled him in such an overwhelmingly powerful way that he fell to the ground. I was overjoyed for Keith and thanked Chris, who left us together to pray some more, giving God all the thanks and praise for what He had done.

However, the immediate change in Keith was something I wasn't prepared for. Whereas he had always put my wants and needs before his own, he now just wanted to spend time with Jesus. He didn't ask me what I wanted to do, or if I minded. He didn't seem to care about me. Off he went to one of the worship tents. I was left alone, feeling somewhat bewildered. What was going on? This is not how it's supposed to be, is it, Jesus? I know this may sound overly dramatic, but I felt as if in some way Keith had just issued me with a certificate of divorce, albeit a spiritual one. I wandered around feeling bereft. I actually recall experiencing what a child must feel when they have lost their parent in a crowded place. People milled all around me, but I was utterly abandoned.

By this time I was panicking, so I stumbled toward a little tent that had been set aside especially for prayer. I fell through the door into what at first appeared to be a void of complete darkness. My eyes adjusted to the lack of light, but I couldn't see much by this time anyway as I was in floods of tears. I was alone again, abandoned again. I slumped to the grassy floor and just wept and wept. As my sobs subsided, I sensed a presence with me. I opened my puffy eyes, but there was no one else in the tent with me. As I closed my eyes I heard Jesus speak to me. His words were simple and gentle, yet they were spoken with absolute authority. He said to me, "Mandy, if I take your husband from you, you will still have Me. If I take your children from you, you will still have Me. Even if I take everything from you, you will still have *Me!* I will never leave or forsake you; I will never abandon you—you are Mine."

Having been reminded of Jesus' words while I sat in this women's meeting, I realized that, despite everything, Jesus is true to His word. I still have *Him.* I was then, and am now, assured of that fact. It is not just a warm, comforting feeling or a wishful thought. It is truth. It sustains me in the present and strengthens me for whatever is to come in my unseen future.

I tell this story to encourage you; you may also be experiencing unexplained suffering. I want to encourage you to look beyond your situation to the fact that your God has emotions too. He weeps when you weep. He too has grieved. He is your suffering Savior. He is the answer to all the world's unanswered questions. So if your suffering leads you away from a belief in Jesus, you allow yourself to be led away from the only hope there is to this universal problem. No other religion or philosophy has an appropriate answer, humanism included; none can supply the hope found only in Jesus and His resurrection.

Scripture points to a future when we will fully understand:

> *For we know in part and we prophesy in part, but when completeness comes, what is in part disappears. When I was a child, I talked like a child, I thought like a child, I reasoned like a child. When I became a man, I put the ways of*

childhood behind me. For now we see only a reflection as in a mirror; then we shall see face to face. Now I know in part; then I shall know fully, even as I am fully known (1 Corinthians 13:9b-12).

Dear friends, now we are children of God, and what we will be has not yet been made known. But we know that when Christ appears, we shall be like him, for we shall see him as he is (1 John 3:2).

In the meantime I have decided to believe that God knows what He is doing. I can wait for that day when:

He will wipe every tear from their eyes. There will be no more death or mourning or crying or pain, for the old order of things has passed away (Revelation 21:4).

For further reading, I can't recommend *Shattered Dreams* by Larry Crabb[2] highly enough. It was a difficult and uncomfortable read, but it changed my thinking about disappointment and suffering. Our God is a good God even though we sometimes don't have the capacity to understand. However, one important question still remains; it is Jesus' question to you today: "Will you trust Me?"

Endnotes

1. Hannah Hurnard, *Hinds Feet on High Places* (Eastbourne, UK: Kingsway Communications Ltd, 1982).

2. Larry Crabb, *Shattered Dreams, Gods Unexpected Path to Joy* (Colorado Springs, CO: WaterBrook Press, 2010).

Chapter 10

Your Personal Invitation

If you yearn to hear God's voice but haven't taken time until now, listen love, you too will hear His voice calling your name. It is His voice and His presence that will satisfy the longing within you that cannot be filled by what the world has to offer. Taking a step into faith is just that—a simple, gentle step, not the dangerous leap you might imagine.

Do you want to step into an embrace that will hold you securely, with a love that is eternal and will never let you go? If you do, then you are only a prayer away from a relationship with the all-powerful Lover of your soul.

Prayer, in its basic form, is just talking to God. If you have trouble forming your own words, but you want to step into relationship with God, you can use the following prayer:

Lord Jesus, I come to You today to say I believe in You. I believe You are God's Son, come to earth to save me. I am a sinner and, I accept that my actions have separated me from God. I know that I cannot save myself. I believe that You lived a perfect life and died on the cross to pay the price for my sins. I believe You rose from the dead and that You are alive.

I repent (turn away) from my past life, all the ungodly choices I have made. I ask that You forgive me, and that in taking all of my sin upon Yourself on the cross, I receive forgiveness.

I ask, Jesus, that You come into my life, come into my heart and live there by Your Holy Spirit. I surrender all of myself (my soul, will, intellect, character and emotions, and my body) to You, and ask that You take control.

I humbly thank You Jesus for what You have done just for me, and that through You my spirit is made alive, my name is written in the Book of Life, and I will be with You eternally. Amen.

If you have just said the words of this prayer for the first time and taken a step of faith into the person and eternal work of Jesus Christ, welcome home, you have entered the family of God Himself. All of Heaven is delighted, and the adventure begins! The journey with Jesus may not always seem easy, but I can promise you one thing—there will be plenty of joy.

Go on, be brave, and tell someone you trust what you have just done. Come every day to sit at Jesus' feet in prayer, and remember that God's Spirit is in you. Get yourself a Bible and start reading about all the wonderful things God has done, is doing, and will do. Begin to take hold of all the promises He has just for you, and don't forget, if you haven't already done so, to go back and finish reading *Gorgeous* and discover just how beautiful you really are!

AFTERWORD

THE LITTLE DANCING FLOWER

A final word of encouragement to you, beautiful one, in the scene that lies before me. I am sitting at the back of the Prayer Room at the International House of Prayer in Kansas City, Missouri, USA, having accepted an offer to accompany my pastor, Silvia Nickelson, on this visit. My trip here and what I am now experiencing are unexpected, having not previously planned to travel to the U.S. It is as if I have been lovingly kidnapped by the Holy Spirit just for the purposes of writing this book for you and to describe to you what I see before me:

> A little girl, no more than five years of age, catches my attention. She has decided to dance as the adults around her sing their worship to Jesus. As if unsure

of herself, she moves hesitantly. She looks around to check whether anyone is looking. No, no one has noticed her. She feels safer now, so she adds a few more steps to her dance. A raised hand directs her body into her first twirl. It was a little ambitious, and she totters a bit, but soon corrects her balance.

With a gulp of courage she now takes a big leap. Her movements are somewhat awkward, and the sudden momentum brings her to her knees. She raises her head and her body follows into its first faltering glide across the floor. She does another spin, this time with greater boldness, her arms held aloft; then she skims the floor in one harmonious action.

Before long this lovely little thing is filling the space she entered. People are watching now, but she is completely unaware of their presence. She is dancing for the One who loves her most, the Father Gardener, His Son, and His Spirit.

As she continues her dance, people are drawn to admire it. Her dance speaks to their hearts, and they hear her unspoken invitation to join the dance with her because she has discovered the One for whom she is dancing. Her shaky, often stumbling beginning is turning into the most graceful act of love pouring naturally out of her, as she receives joy from the Lord of the dance and gives Him joy in return.

I am like that little girl; I have stepped out onto the stage of life and am learning to dance like the flowers do in the meadows. Come join me in the dance. You don't have to know all the steps beforehand. You don't have to be perfect. Your individual style of dance will develop the more you just learn to be a flower in the Garden Heart of God.

About the Author

Mandy Muckett lives in Basel, Switzerland, with her husband, Keith, and daughters, Georgia and Sydney. She is on the leadership team of her home church, Oikos International, Basel. She also serves as a Speaker Ambassador for the Child Sponsorship charity, Compassion, Schweiz and works with Rahab, the Salvation Army's outreach in Basel's Red-Light district.

Mandy regularly speaks, using spiritual examples from Gorgeous to encourage women to see themselves as God sees them, free from the judgement of others. She serves as a Spiritual Mother and enjoys sharing the treasures and freedoms she has learnt following Jesus.

You may contact Mandy Muckett at:

Email: info@mandymuckett.com
Web site: www.mandymuckett.com
Facebook Page: Mandy Muckett - Author
Twitter Account: @MandyMuckett

Made in the USA
Coppell, TX
15 January 2022